If you aren't interested in seeing our world reached for Christ, I suggest you stay away from Dan Jarvis's new book, *Commissioned*. Filled with compelling stories of Christians in Asia who are daily living out the Great Commission, this book will challenge your current lifestyle and encourage you to step into full obedience to Christ. I especially like the short, practical challenges at the end of each chapter. The inspiring stories alone are worth picking up this book of modern saints who are following Jesus regardless of the cost.

—DAVE BUTTS, President of Harvest Prayer Ministries and Chairman of Americ's National Prayer Committee

Sadly, the incredible accounts of people encountering God that we find on the pages of our Bible read like fairy tales or the histories of times long past. Even when we believe them, they seem somehow beyond the realm of possibility for the present age. But Dan Jarvis takes us to a place where stunning miracles and rapid advancement of the gospel are happening on a scale that boggles the mind. His eye-witness report will dramatically expand what Christians in the West might expect from God right here and right now.

—DEL FEHSENFELD III, Senior Editor of *Revive* Magazine, Life Action Ministries

Even though the world is at our doorstep, most people raised in Western culture live in a small way. Our ambitions (if we have them) tend toward material advance, pleasures of the moment, securing a retirement. But, every now and then, we stumble upon a larger, exhilarating, mind-bending world of adventure, life and death, dreams and challenges that change the course of lifetimes. We find ourselves not just reading about, but actually becoming a part of a story of incredible hope that reaches into our deepest being and gives us a taste of what it means to be used of God. That's the world of this book; this is the world that waits for each of us. I know. I've been there. I've seen it. I've been changed by it. And, I long to be even more a part of the unfolding story. You will, too. You will never be satisfied with the incidental again.

—**JIM LYON,** General Director of the Church of God, Anderson, Indiana

India is so vast and ancient. We often remember it in negative terms – a religious country that is very mystical and animistic, many gods that reflect the sensual desires of men, a social caste system that condemns a large segment of the populace to perpetual squalor and despair. But to judge a people as such and then close the book on them is to turn your back on mankind and to miss the heart of God. This is where Sam Stephens steps up and in the name of Jesus, makes a difference. He saw something different; he saw what India could be when Christ became their focus. For generations the Stephens family has reached out in love to bring the gospel of Jesus to the masses of India. When I met Sam, I met a man who genuinely loves his people. He has sacrificed and served them with abandon. From his efforts and the efforts of IGL, thousands of churches have grown up. The message proclaimed by the apostle Thomas in the first century has begun to flourish once again in the heart of India.

—**Dr. RICHARD FISHER,** former Regional Director and Professor for Moody Bible Institute

This is undoubtedly India's moment in the great history of the kingdom of God. To see it is to believe it, and Dan Jarvis has come back a believer. His personal journey through the spiritual heart of India is a wonderful testament to God's power in action and His church in motion. Let this powerful account inspire you and more importantly, motivate you to action! Now is the time to join the greatest missionary movement in history.

—**BRAM FLORIA,** Producer and Director of Compassion Radio

Dan has a curiosity that keeps him restless and dissatisfied with "normal" church. When he discovered what God was doing in India, he had to go see it for himself. This book is more than a report of what he found. It's a charge to those who love and lead Christ's church in the West to curiously ask, "God, would you replicate in my church, in my lifetime, the same kind of movement that is bringing such spiritual growth and health to the churches of Asia?" May the Lord use this book to make us all dissatisfied with "normal" church until we experience a movement of spiritual awakening, a new normal!

—**TRENT GRIFFITH,** Pastor of Harvest Bible Chapel, Granger, Indiana

In an age of declining Christian influence in the West, the Spirit of God is doing amazing things in Asia. *Commissioned* is a timely book that expands our vision of how great and vast and alive is the kingdom of God. The stories of what God is doing in India and Sri Lanka are like accounts straight from the book of Acts. The American church needs to read this book and be challenged to consider the methods for evangelism and church planting that are actually working and succeeding in Asia. This book challenges our laziness, apathy, and low expectations. *Commissioned* will rekindle a fire in your soul for evangelism and discipleship.

—ISRAEL WAYNE, Author and Conference Speaker,
Director of Family Renewal

Books transport me to places I could never go. *Commissioned* not only grabbed my interest from the very beginning, it held on to me until the last page was turned. Because it is real and contemporary the book becomes that much more compelling. What God is doing in the nation of India is astonishing. Read about it and let the amazement bring joy to your soul and praise to the One who has orchestrated it all. It is the next best thing to being there. I know, because I have seen it. I have walked with Sam Stephens. I have wept with him. I have prayed with him. *Commissioned* will bring you as close as you can come without traveling to India yourself. Read it and then, "come and see."

—JIM COLLEDGE, Founding Pastor of Christ Community
Chapel in Hudson, Ohio and Pastor of
The Chapel in North Canton

Commissioned is the amazing story of the incredible work of God in India. It is a page-turner that reads like the opening chapters of Acts. It caused me to want to be a part of what

God is doing in India, as well as to see Him do those works in my nation again. This would be a great small group study for a church that wants to ignite a new hunger for global missions and fuel a desire for revival in their own nation.

—**GREGG SIMMONS,** Revivalist with Life Action Ministries and former Pastor of Church at the Cross, Grapevine, Texas

I have traveled the roads of India for over twenty-five years, working closely with India Gospel League. You will find in these pages the story of how God has taken a small seed of faith and vastly increased the His kingdom. Dan Jarvis has captured the essence of what God can do when His children walk by faith and not by sight. You will be amazed by the faith of the people and the work of God in response. This is a book of actual accounts, highlighting the lives of those who have been commissioned by and for Christ in their world. You will be both blessed and challenged by this witness.

—**CLAUDE ROBOLD,** Pastor of New Covenant Church, Middletown, Ohio

Being a fellow traveler to India with Dan, I have personally seen him engage with the culture. Dan is not a casual observer, but an in-depth investigative reporter. To understand and experience the rapid advance of the kingdom of God, this book is a must-read.

— **ROGER KORSTEN,** Pastor of Highland Sixth Presbyterian Church, Highland Heights, Ohio

Commissioned is exactly what the church in North America needs—a fresh perspective, a book-of-Acts reality, a challenge to fully and finally engage in the the advancement of Christ's kingdom. Perhaps as we pray for revival in the West, we should take note of the seeds of spiritual awakening springing up in the East? The stories of sacrifice and commitment that Dan has collected from remote villages and tropical jungles will inspire you not only to believe, but to take action. By the time you set this book down, the Great Commission will no longer be for others, for professionals, for missionaries in faraway lands. It will be for you."

- BYRON PAULUS, President of Life Action Ministries and co-author of *OneCry: A Nationwide Call for Spiritual Awakening*

COMMISSIONED

HOW GOD IS CHANGING LIVES,
TRANSFORMING NATIONS,
AND INVOLVING YOU

DAN JARVIS

PUBLISHED BY

Commissioned

Printed in the United States of America.

Published by India Gospel League, North America
1521 Georgetown Road, Suite 305
Hudson, OH 44236
www.iglworld.org

Design and layout by Flood Creative,
Buchanan, Michigan.

Scripture quotations are from *The Holy Bible,
English Standard Version* (ESV), copyright © 2001
by Crossway, a publishing ministry of Good News
Publishers. Used by permission. All rights reserved.

ISBN 978-1-934718-41-4

DEDICATION

To those who are giving their all for the gospel, facing danger and staying faithful. Only the Great Day will reveal how much they sacrificed for God's kingdom, and how many souls were introduced to Christ as a result.

With special thanks to John, Karen, Ellen, Sam, Melissa, Tim, Kim, Aaron, Kathryn, Kate, Prag, Melvin, Paul Raj, Becky, Jegan, another John, Danny, Benny, and many others who offered their skills, stories, and time toward the completion of this book. In eternity, my friends, let's compare notes about all that God has done through this project for His glory.

TABLE OF CONTENTS

FOREWORD

I was unprepared for the experience. An invitation from Sam Stephens had come to me months earlier to speak at a conference held at Sharon Gardens, a ministry center of India Gospel League (IGL). With each hour of the long flight and bus trip, I was becoming further removed from familiar Western culture, on this, my first visit to India. Thrilled and eager, I alighted from the bus to meet Sam.

Sam wasn't the only person ready to greet me. Over two hundred children, housed at Sharon Gardens, joined in the welcome. These precious little ones performed a greeting of song and dance, and I learned from Sam that many of them had been brought in by their impoverished parents because they knew that their children could be fed, educated, and loved in this special place.

The next morning I saw a school where over 900 students are being educated, a fully accredited community college, a job training center, an agricultural facility for teaching improved farming efforts, and a cancer hospital complete with state-of-the-art surgical suites and hospice care.

Education, economic development, health care, spiritual instruction, and nurture—it's all there.

The tour left me speechless, but not tearless. I had caught a glimpse of the kingdom of heaven and was instructed by it. I hadn't made it to "church" yet, but had run head on into God's work in the world.

In my Western church upbringing, I had picked up the assumption that God's primary work in the world is building His church. I was taught to look for God at church, during times of worship, praise, and sermons. Then, in those worship services, people were challenged to take God back into their homes, workplaces, schools, and neighborhoods.

But the truth was—and is—we don't have to take God anywhere. *He's already there.* In fact, it is God who wants to take *us* somewhere! To where His heart is breaking. To the world.

The world is where we should look for God. After all, it's what God gave His only begotten Son for (according to Jesus, who should know something about this!). Church-centric thinking can shrink-wrap God's concerns down to His being focused on what happens during Sunday morning services. But a kingdom focus leads us to something greater than that: into partnering with God in His redemptive mission in the *world*. That means everything damaged by sin is currently being redeemed and restored by God.

This is the mission that God has asked us to join. Whatever matters to God ought to matter to us. The world—all aspects of it—is important to Him. None of our artificial and superficial categories of sacred/secular can hold up with this understanding of what God is up to. We cannot hide inside church walls or crouch behind theological barriers in order to practice a religion that does not love God at every level and love our neighbors as ourselves.

I finally did make it to "church" in India. It was the dedication of a building constructed by a congregation in a village. The structure is not called a "church." The congregations associated with IGL call the facilities where they gather "Life Centers." After all, *life* is what Jesus promised to bring to us. On that Sunday, we dedicated the Life Center to the village for whatever purpose it could serve to bring life—as a school, a medical clinic, a job training center, and, yes, a place for Jesus followers to gather.

For Sam and the people of IGL, "church" is a way of being *in* the world. It is centered on kingdom living, demonstrating the good news of God's grace, and loving intentions for human beings who bear His image. Maybe this is why spending a week with them was like living a week in the book of Acts.

Please turn the page to start your own journey with India Gospel League. You may or may not go to South Asia. But you *will* wind up in the world. And you will run head on into God.

—**Reggie McNeal,** Leadership Network

CHAPTER 1

WHAT IS GOD DOING?

It was a terrible accident. Melvin, a third-grade boy from India's Maharashtra region, was on his way to a Hindu temple with his father and uncle. All three were injured badly when they lost control of their vehicle. Melvin and his uncle recovered at the hospital over the next two weeks, but the father didn't. Instead, the father's skin turned red, and the family exhausted its money on medical testing. The results were grim.

During his hospitalization, the father had contracted leprosy.

Melvin explains what happened next, as this hopeless, painful reality set in:

> My father was very stubborn. After he was released from the hospital, he kept going to the Hindu temple, even though someone had told him that Jesus could help. "Give your life to Christ!" a Christian pastor implored, "and ask Him to heal you." But my father resisted. Finally, in desperation, he went to the Christian church and asked for prayer.
>
> The pastor prayed and then looked at my father in the eyes. "You will be healed, Sir."

Within fifteen days, the leprosy was *gone*.

From then on, of course, our whole lives started to change. We got rid of our family idols. We started learning from God's Word and trusting in Jesus Christ. And as a young boy, I gave my life to ministry. As soon as I was of age, I went to Bible school to become a pastor.

Melvin's story was just beginning. To date, he has served in three different regions of India, preaching the gospel and planting churches.

"God has worked mighty miracles," he continued. "People with cancer and thyroid problems have been healed. Even a dead child was raised to life in a village. These miracles have opened doors for the gospel."

As I listened to Pastor Melvin, I couldn't help but ask questions:

"Pastor Melvin, as I travel in India, I hear stories like yours frequently. In areas that have never been touched by the gospel before, God works miracles to show the people His power over idols. But sometimes miracles don't happen. What do you say to those people you pray for who aren't healed?"

This young pastor, who looked to be no more than 35 years old, never broke eye contact with me. In a soft, confident voice, he gave his answer. "I say to them, 'In His time, God makes everything beautiful, so have patience. The Bible says He is a loving Father. Any earthly father would try his best to heal his child, and I believe God will do this for you. In the meantime, you must believe. He is working out everything according to Romans 8:28.'"

Knowing I would return home from my trip to India and begin working on this book, I asked Melvin what words of encouragement he might have for Christians across the world who would hear his story. He said, "Jesus is the same yesterday and today and forever. What worked 2,000 years ago is still working now. So be faithful to the Lord. When I was called to the ministry, I believe the Spirit of God said, 'There is no turning back.'"

Pastor Melvin's story reminded me of what Oliver Holmes said, "A mind, once expanded by a new idea, can never return to its original dimensions." Once you see what God is doing, once you hear His call, *there is,* as Pastor Melvin said so well, *no turning back.*

WHAT'S YOUR STORY?

Most people live with their heads down, focused on their work, a tiny screen in their hand, or the next step they are about to take. Some are so engaged with the "here and now" that they never look up to see what God is doing around them, around their church, and around the world. Others would rather argue the finer points of doctrine than live and experience the truths being debated. Admittedly, I was that way once. But no longer.

What if I told you there are thousands of young churches scattered across India today, on the very front lines of Great Commission fulfillment, experiencing the power and presence of Christ in ways similar to Pastor Melvin's story?

What if told you that in South Asia, one of the least-reached regions on earth (where millions have yet to even hear the name of Jesus, let alone the gospel), God has sparked a movement of spiritual growth that rivals any in history?

What if I told you tens of thousands of leaders like Pastor Melvin are boldly preaching the gospel in the midst of persecution?

How would you respond?

If you're anything like I was before I saw and heard first-hand what God is doing in India, your attitude (unspoken but felt) is something like this: You suspect God is doing amazing, impressive, joyous things to redeem broken, sad, and sinful people, but you aren't privy to them. You have too much to do. Your work or family life is too demanding. Your church activities occasionally yield fruit, but they are a far cry from what Paul, Barnabas, or Silas experienced.

You've grown comfortable, assuming such outpourings of the Holy Spirit are, for some reason, not yours to claim. Your vision is too clouded by the compromises you've made and sins that lurk in your own heart. And yet, you'd like to see the kingdom of God in its fullness. You'd love to be a part of the larger purpose God has for this world. And you'd like to stand in front of Christ on Judgment Day to hear Him proclaim, "Well done, good and faithful servant!"

But all of it seems a step away from reality. Your reality. And it all seems so distant. Possibly you think the great miracles of God's power in the lives of famous Old Testament characters and the book-of-Acts generation are relegated to their respective historical eras. Or perhaps you even know about God's glory appearing in faraway lands in recent days. But, so far, *not in your life*. Not in your church.

This book isn't all about miracles, though you'll read about many more in the pages to follow. And it isn't just about what God is doing in India. Rather, this is a book about completing the Great Commission, and doing so in our lifetime. In these pages you'll meet some of the characters God is using in this unfolding story, but even more, you will encounter the *living Jesus,* the One who is at work today to *change* lives, *redeem* the lost, and *transform* communities. If you're willing, you can join Jesus in His work.

So what's your story?

"I'm too busy."

"I'm not gifted enough."

"I have too many responsibilities."

"I've already sinned too much, so God can't use me."

"People wouldn't understand."

"I don't know where to begin."

What would you like it to be instead?

NO MORE EXCUSES

Any excuse still lingering in my heart was put to rest when I stepped off a plane in tropical Bangalore, India, and into the lives of faithful men and women who serve in an indigenous ministry called India Gospel League (IGL). These individuals are part of a growing movement to take the gospel into the rural villages of India—remote regions (far from large cities) where millions live and die without ever even hearing the name of Jesus once in their lifetime. From IGL's "barefoot pastors" who literally walk beyond where the road ends, I've learned more than I could ever recount about prayer, about sacrifice, about life, about the gospel, about the power of the Holy Spirit, about the change that our world needs today, and about the condition of my own Christian life.

I've had the privilege to travel to India several times in the past few years to assist IGL in training village pastors. On each occasion, I was enamored with the culture, in love with the people, spiced out by the food, and genuinely excited by the growth of churches in a region of the world that most certainly qualifies as "the end of the earth" (Acts 1:8). And on each occasion, I boarded the plane back home with a heart full of refreshed passion for Christ, a revived desire to follow Him wherever He may lead.

WHY INDIA?

Nearly 1.3 billion people live in India and the neighboring island of Sri Lanka. That's three times the population of the U.S. in a country about one-third the geographic size. Among these precious souls, only a slight percentage are Bible-believing Christians—in fact, as of November 2013, more than 90% of India's population lives in unreached people groups. *That means there are more than one billion people in India alone who have little or no access to the gospel!* (The Joshua Project tracks statistical information on people groups across the world, and can offer many more specifics regarding the unreached areas of South Asia: www.JoshuaProject.net.)

The largest percentage of the population follows the teachings of Hinduism. Others follow Islam or Buddhism. Still others are in tribal groups with animist beliefs. Most of these one billion unreached souls are illiterate farmers who live in abject poverty, making a living by working in the fields and surviving on meager (sometimes scarce) food. Most don't have a Christian church in their village. Some don't have the Bible translated into their language. Millions haven't even heard Jesus' name, let alone His gospel.

But the Holy Spirit is using India Gospel League, and other Christian groups in the area, to change that.

The first time I landed on the Indian subcontinent, the stories I'd read in missionary biographies suddenly leapt from grayscale history into present, living-color reality. I was about to stand in front of hundreds of Indian Christian workers—men and women who were giving their all for Christ—to train them and encourage them in God's Word. And though my formal theological training in the States supposedly qualified me to be their instructor, I would quickly realize I needed to be schooled by them also. They were the ones on the front lines of the kingdom's advance; they were the ones experiencing God's power in the present; they were the ones facing persecution, poverty, and earthly loss as a result of their surrender to Jesus Christ.

Yes, I would shake hands and join in prayer with men and women whose stories belong in a series of "biographies of great Christians." Except they weren't "great" by the world's definition. They weren't all that different from you or me. During my time with them, we would laugh at jokes together, wonder how our kids would turn out, and swap personal prayer requests and share photos of our families. What set these men and women apart as "great Christians" in my mind was their full-life answer to the call of the gospel. They were *living* what most of us only talk about!

On the outside we had a few differences. I'm 6'6", and most people in India are, shall we say, a bit shorter. I look like I have been well fed for most of my life, while most of them are lean. My skin is light and rosy, while theirs is darker and hardened by the Indian sun. My clothes are the latest in Western fashion, while theirs are more basic and indigenous to their culture.

My background couldn't be any more foreign to theirs. I'd grown up in a comfortable world of grocery stores and electronic gadgets, middle-class American houses, and easy access to everything from lattes to television. My family had turned to Christ from a secular worldview and started attending an established, 150-year-old congregation in my northeast Ohio hometown. I had become a Christian at an early age, after much exposure to the gospel, and I'd enjoyed the privileges of an advanced education and opportunities to earn multiple degrees and certifications. My personal income was commensurate with my abilities and more than adequate for my personal and family needs.

The background of my Indian friends told a different story. Some had grown up in rural villages, far from the world of new cars and modern, 2,000-square-foot homes, in agrarian communities filled with the hustle of oxen and open-air marketplaces, small motorcycles, and thatch roofs. Many had encountered the gospel for the first time when a traveling church planter visited their village and shared how Christ's power was superior to that of the idols their family had worshipped for generations. Those who trusted in Christ often faced persecution from family and friends—at least, rejection and suspicion; at most, physical harm and violent threats. And, in the absence of an established congregation and a church building, they had banded together with other fledging new believers to form the nucleus of a new church—often to become the first Christian presence *ever* in that community.

At first glance, it might be tempting for an observer to note how much "more" I had than they did. More money. More cultural acceptance of my worldview. More amenities at my church. More freedom to worship God without persecution. More educational and technological resources at my disposal. But I would soon learn how out of whack that perspective really was. They had something "more" that I had only read about, something I had wished for—something I knew I both wanted and needed.

They had the power and presence of God in their everyday lives.

I don't say this to dismiss the good work God has done in my life, my church, or even in my country. I've seen the Lord do some amazing things. But what I have witnessed in the lives of these Indian brothers and sisters is different. And I've concluded that if it is possible to learn a few lessons from them, I'm all ears. I want to know and experience as much of God as a human being can, and they are an open door to gain that experience. When I see Him at work in rural villages of India in ways I never dreamed possible in my own context, I want to discern *how* He does it. And *why*. And, by God's grace, *how I can participate*.

AN INVITATION

This book is an invitation. It is not just to *learn about* how God is at work in a different culture but to *really experience* the Christian life. A life defined by God's purposes instead of our own. A life that looks at eternity instead of just this world. A life that, very practically, is a part of the Great Commission's completion in our generation.

The invitation isn't necessarily for you to hop aboard a 747 and cross the ocean, nor is it to seek out some undiscovered "new truth" from a mysterious place. Instead, it is to think with me about the Great Commission by looking at what God is doing in one region of the world, to lift up your eyes to the great harvest God is bringing in and see yourself as part of the scene. It is also an invitation to take a fresh look into the pages of God's Word without dismissing God's power as "for another time" or "for another place."

Are we not serving the God who parted the Red Sea? The God who brought fire out of the clear blue sky to burn the sacrifice of Elijah? The God who routed the world's most powerful armies and healed the world's most feared diseases? Are we not serving the God who raised our Lord Jesus from the dead?

Indeed we are! And God's power is no less for us *now* than it was for them *then*. The twenty-first-century church has the same access to God's power as the first-century church did. Jesus Christ really is the same yesterday, today, and forever. Do you believe this? And, more to the point, are you experiencing this?

Consider Paul's prayer for the Ephesians, that they would understand "the immeasurable greatness of His power toward us who believe, according to the working of His great might that He worked in Christ when He raised Him from the dead and seated Him at His right hand in the heavenly places" (Eph. 1:19-20). Consider his words as he charged that young church: "Now to Him who is able to do far more abundantly than all that we ask or think, according to the power at work within us, to Him be glory in the church and in Christ Jesus throughout all generations, forever and ever. Amen" (Eph. 3:20-21).

Do those verses describe the cry of your heart?

God's power isn't a one-time show. He didn't *just* part the Red Sea for one generation or raise Jesus from the dead for another. He didn't *just* do beyond what "those people, long ago, over there" could ask or think. No. His work is for and in all generations. The same "great might" can define our lives, our families, and even our communities. Every ounce of power that was available in the days of Gideon or Isaiah or the apostle Paul is available to people like you and me today.

Will you accept my invitation? Would you like to see what God is doing in Asia today? And would you like to learn what it means to really live out the Great Commission?

_____

Note: At the conclusion of every chapter, you'll find a social media prompt—the first few words of a suggested post or status update you can use to share what you're learning, challenge your friends, and connect with others across the world who are engaged in God's call. Each SHARE IT is a starter idea, so be as creative as you'd like! You can tag any quotes or comments regarding this book with #Commissioned, then click the tag to see what others are learning. India Gospel League's Twitter name is @IndiaGL, and our hashtag for news is #iglworld. On Facebook, you can like India Gospel League to join our community.

DISCUSS IT

Thus far in your Christian life, how has God showcased His mighty power to you?

If God's power were somehow poured out in a new way through your church, how do you think your community would react? How about your personal friends? You?

When you hear about God's power being displayed in other countries, what emotions do you feel?

ACT ON IT

Begin with this prayer: "Lord, I'm willing to open Your Word with fresh eyes to see how Your mighty power can work in and through me. And as I read these stories from India, please build my faith. Grow my vision. May the spark of Great Commission calling light a new fire in my soul, for Your glory."

SHARE IT

I'm reading #Commissioned from India Gospel League, and my prayer is . . .

Welcome to India! The nation is a dazzling combination of modern and ancient, of ox carts and buses sharing the same road.

The author encouraging a village congregation as they dedicate their new Life Center—a place for worship, education, and community service.

A common silhouette against the evening sky; a woman carries water to her family dwelling a few kilometers away.

CHAPTER 2

HOW IT BEGAN

The final words of instruction Jesus gave His followers are recorded in Acts 1, and they mark a grand beginning for the Christian movement across the world.

"But you will receive power when the Holy Spirit has come upon you, and you will be my witnesses in Jerusalem and in all Judea and Samaria, and to the end of the earth." And when he had said these things, as they were looking on, he was lifted up, and a cloud took him out of their sight. And while they were gazing into heaven as he went, behold, two men stood by them in white robes, and said, "Men of Galilee, why do you stand looking into heaven? This Jesus, who was taken up from you into heaven, will come in the same way as you saw him go into heaven" (Acts 1:8-11).

I don't blame the disciples for being stunned into silent gawking at what they had just experienced. Not only had they met and eaten with the resurrected Savior, but He had just handed them a worldwide commission and then risen to disappear from their sight in the clouds!

A tax collector. A few fishermen. A few other "average people." Now entrusted with the message that would be the hope of the world! Now commissioned to carry Christ's very words to the city of Jerusalem. And to the surrounding regions of Judea and Samaria. And to the very ends of the earth!

They weren't asked to tackle this magnificent mission on their own, by their own resolve or ingenuity. No, this gospel that would move across the world, this movement that would change *everything,* would be empowered by God Himself. Jesus had said, "You will receive power when the Holy Spirit has come upon you, and you will be My witnesses . . ." (Acts 1:8).

It is obvious in Scripture that God enjoys using the humble, the unlikely, the "foolish things of this world" (like you and me) to bring about changes that turn everything upside down for His purposes. Such was the case in the book of Acts, when a rag-tag band of disciples unleashed the gospel, in the power of the Holy Spirit, upon an unsuspecting, yet very needy, world.

That was then. This is now.

Jesus is at work, just as He always has been. And He uses people you and I couldn't imagine to do things we wouldn't believe possible—except it is happening. Nowhere is it more evident to me than in South Asia, where all the "wisdom" of the world can't heal a broken life *but the gospel can.*

MEET SAM STEPHENS

Sam Stephens is a humble Indian man who God is using to foster massive church-planting and humanitarian advances in his nation and the island of Sri Lanka. Sam has taught me more about living the gospel than anyone else I've encountered. From casting leadership vision to training Bible students, from nurturing needy widows to caring for lost orphans, Sam lives exactly what he preaches.

Let's pick up Rev. Stephens' story in 1992. He had been entrusted with the leadership of India Gospel League, a regional ministry in the state of Tamil Nadu, South India, reaching out on what now would be considered a "small" scale to the rural areas surrounding his hometown, the village of Salem. Sam's father, and his father before him, had assumed leadership of this same group, a team of itinerant evangelists committed to taking the gospel into villages where there was no established Christian witness. Medical, educational, and economic help followed. Sam had already served for years as a traveling evangelist and pastor before the passing of his father, before the mantle of leadership fell on his shoulders.

Nestled in the midst of tropical mountains, swaying palms, and dire poverty, India Gospel League's "mission base," located on the outskirts of Salem in an area called Sharon, appeared as a blossom of hope in the midst of the despair and neediness surrounding it. The base, called Sharon Gardens, at first simply consisted of Sam's family home and a small orphanage for destitute children. Sam would hold meetings there with a networked group of pastors and evangelists involved in India Gospel League's efforts to pray and seek God's direction.

At one such gathering, the Lord revealed to Sam a new direction for the ministry. Rather than only "traditional" evangelism and services to meet the needs of the people, he and those working with him were to commit themselves to a multiplication approach for *church planting and discipleship.* After all, if areas were evangelized but self-sustaining village churches weren't established, how would new disciples grow in their faith? More importantly, if new believers were not being trained to share the gospel with others and to take the gospel to surrounding villages, how could the small group of networked pastors possibly take the gospel to the more than 600,000 rural villages in India?

Standing before the group of about two hundred gathered that day, Rev. Stephens asked them to make a radical shift in their ministry plans. Rather than the traditional roles of pastoring or evangelism, would they instead work to establish *new* congregations? Many responded favorably, despite the great risks and costs involved.

Imagine: if each of these pastors and evangelists were to take on the challenge to establish at least one new congregation in a new village within a year's time, how many more villages would have a church community established? And through those new churches, the blessings of the gospel could flow out for years to come! And if believers from each of those new congregations were to be trained to share their faith so they could help establish congregations of believers in their nearby villages—well, anyone could do the math. It was a brilliant vision, one only God could have placed before Sam and his band of itinerant evangelists.

VISION 2000

With prayer, Sam and those gathered with him that day agreed to what seemed like an impossible goal—to somehow evangelize and plant churches in *one thousand villages* before the end of the year 2000. They dubbed their movement "Vision 2000," looking ahead in faith to the year 2000 when they could celebrate the victory of a thousand villages finally having a Christian light established in them.

What would constitute a church? Sam and the leadership agreed that a church could be "counted" once it reached twenty baptized adult believers worshipping weekly. Many churches would, of course, grow larger, and still others would spring into what we might call "multi-site" congregations.

And so the Vision 2000 movement was launched, and the results were phenomenal. God was at work through their faith. Lives were changed, the lost redeemed, communities transformed, and people mobilized to plant new churches and actively seek out more villages that needed to hear about Jesus. Established churches then branched out to nearby areas. Some pastors felt specific callings from God to move into totally unreached areas. India Gospel League's efforts multiplied.

When the group of leaders met again a year later, it became apparent that the stated goal was *too small*. More pastors were joining the vision, and young churches were spawning even more young churches. Within a few years, Vision 2000 was revised to prayerfully target the planting of *five thousand* new churches by the turn of the millennium!

But even that goal would prove insufficient. A wildfire had been sparked. Churches planted churches, which planted churches. Pastors became church planters, and trained leaders trained more leaders. Other pastors, who had been operating independently, joined the movement and adopted Vision 2000 as well.

By the time Sam and the IGL leadership met to rejoice in the year 2000, more than 20,000 new village congregations had been established!

Twenty thousand. And that was only the beginning of what God was about to do, and of what God continues to do today.

Within a few years, the momentum had spread beyond the southern India state of Tamil Nadu, into central and north India, and then across the Gulf of Mannar to the island nation of Sri Lanka. Regional leaders were appointed, and in Sri Lanka, local leadership was put into place under the name "Island Gospel League." The meaning of "IGL" grew, and, as I'll share later, it continues to grow, really becoming a sort of "international gospel league" to call people from many cultures into the gospel life!

By the year 2014, through the Vision 2000 movement and India Gospel League's leadership, more than 70,000 congregations have been established and growing – most of them in villages that previously had no Christian presence.

Now pause for a moment and consider: all of this good news is from *one* of *multiple* networks planting churches in South Asia! There are other mission groups that could report great multiplication as well!

INDIA GOSPEL LEAGUE'S COMMISSION

God is doing something today that the missionaries of old could only prayerfully dream of. He is bringing about the fulfillment of the Great Commission in our generation. What's happening in India is evidence. How is He doing it? Through the sacrifice and faith of "average people," He is turning this region upside down!

Today IGL and the Vision 2000 movement provide education and training for thousands of pastors and tens of thousands of young people, gospel teaching for more than 600,000 children annually, medicine for the sick, strategy for regional outreaches, buildings for church plants, clean water wells in villages, job training, orphan care, and much more.

Elementary and secondary schools, a nursing school, and a community college have been built and are transforming the lives of thousands, many formerly illiterate. Economic development strategies are changing isolated villages into centers of productivity for goods and services. A cancer hospital at Sharon Gardens as well as smaller village hospitals and clinics offer hope for the sick where there was none. And not only has the Sharon Gardens mission base grown to include a large conference center for pastoral training, but mission bases like it are being established throughout South Asia.

OUR COMMISSION

While IGL is completely led and run by Indians local to the needs, language, and culture, they have made a pathway available for people anywhere in the world to partner with and pray for this expanding work. That's where you and I come into the picture. We can literally be part of what is happening there.

In the chapters that follow, I will show you what, when, and how. I can't help but remember what Jesus said in Matthew 24:14, "And this gospel of the kingdom will be proclaimed throughout the whole world as a testimony to all nations, and then the end will come." And in Revelation, John reported seeing multitudes from "every tribe, tongue and nation." And as far back as the blessing of Abraham, God promised that through Christ "all the families of the nations shall be blessed."

Surely, as Rev. Stephens is fond of saying, "This is God's time for India!" And God Himself has commissioned you and me, along with our brothers and sisters on the other side of the world, to be a part of what He is doing.

Occasionally I run into believers in the West who don't really "get" the Great Commission. They know it exists, but they don't feel much personal ownership of it. They haven't met someone like Sam Stephens, they haven't seen or felt the power of God as it is evident in India, or they haven't yet captured the essence of what our earthly lifetimes are really about.

In India, no one had to tell me what to think about the gospel work. I saw it. And I'm suggesting that you can see it too. In India? Perhaps. In your nation? Prayerfully, yes. In your church family? Sure. In your own personal life? Of course!

Think of it this way: *Your heart is beating today because the Great Commission is not yet complete.* If God has called you to be in His family, He has also called you to be His ambassador to the world. And whether you are a village pastor in Kerala, India, or a housewife in Cleveland, Ohio, the promises of God's power and presence are yours to claim. The Commission is yours to live.

Jesus said, "All authority in heaven and on earth has been given to me. Go therefore and make disciples of all nations, baptizing them in the name of the Father and of the Son and of the Holy Spirit, teaching them to observe all that I have commanded you. And behold, I am with you always, to the end of the age" (Matthew 28:18-20).

After His resurrection, when Jesus sat down with His disciples and opened their minds so they could understand the Scriptures, where did He direct their attention? To the Commission! To the worldwide vision of God to build a kingdom family from Eden to Ararat to Israel to Jerusalem to your house to my house and to the rural villages of India! He said,

> These are my words that I spoke to you while I was still with you, that everything written about me in the Law of Moses and the Prophets and the Psalms must be fulfilled. . . . Thus it is written, that the Christ should suffer and on the third day rise from the dead, and that repentance and forgiveness of sins should be proclaimed in his name to all nations, beginning in Jerusalem. You are witnesses of these things. And behold, I am sending the promise of my Father upon you (Luke 24:44-49).

I hope, in the course of time, you have the same honor I have had to meet and even travel alongside Sam Stephens and the IGL team as they forge ahead with this gospel advance in South Asia. But even more, I pray that you'll encounter the risen Christ just as His disciples did—that you will set your heart to serve and love Him; that you will adopt His mission as your own. Then you too will be among the voices across the world proclaiming His love, showcasing His glory, and preparing the way for His eternal kingdom.

There is nothing that matters more. There is no reason to wait, to linger, or to "stare into the sky." Jesus left us with one primary responsibility. One job to do. One mission to accomplish. And He's given us all the power we need.

———————————

DISCUSS IT

What would happen where you live if Christian congregations started multiplying exponentially, as they have in South Asia?

With a church planting movement growing as fast as Vision 2000 and IGL, what dangers can you foresee in all the positive reports?

To what extent would you say the Great Commission is *your* job? Who else do you know with this same point of view?

ACT ON IT

Contact someone you know or have heard of who you think really lives out the Great Commission. Ask: "How did you come to Christ? How did you start sharing your faith? What motivates your interest in missions? What steps would you recommend for me?"

SHARE IT

I want to share God's love with the world by . . .

Rev. Sam Stephens is the president of India Gospel League, pictured here in his office in Salem, Tamil Nadu.

Girls attending school at Sharon Gardens, where hundreds are cared for and educated by IGL staff, based on the provision of child sponsors.

Pastors and leaders from across India come to Salem to receive training and encouragement for the work ahead.

CHAPTER 3

LOST EYES, OPEN HEARTS

J esus stood in the temple and said, "The Spirit of the Lord is upon me, because He has anointed me to proclaim good news to the poor" (Luke 4:18). What did He mean, what did poverty look like then, and what do His words here have to do with us today?

One striking feature of Indian life, be it in the city or the countryside, is how poor "the poor" really are. Many villagers live on what amounts to a dollar per day; they farm their own land and subsist on meager minimums. True, some Indians, mostly in the large cities, have risen up and joined the great "development" of the developing world, forging forward to a new prosperity that is outwardly changing India. But such modernization also costs something; many cultural aspects are changing.

But most of the nation still lives in the villages, not the cities. And most of them hail from lower castes, meaning that that the "cards are stacked against them" in every aspect of life: education, friendships, business, even self-image. The caste system (which can no longer be enforced legally yet persists informally) is an ancient pecking order that bears some similarity to racism, but the roots go even deeper. It used to be (and still may be in some places), when a birth certificate was issued, the baby's caste classification was indicated.

The cultural stigma of caste is certainly alive and well in rural India today, and in many cases caste affiliation can be deduced by a person's physical features. Of course, birth in a small village means everyone in the village knows the lineage of the baby, an inescapable reality as long as the individual lives and works in the area. If a baby is born into a poor family (as a Dalit, for example), that child's future is already set.

Due to Hindu religious assumptions regarding *karma*, being born into one of the lower castes means assuming a station in life marked by humiliation and degradation. And those unfortunate enough to be born among the Dalits (the "untouchables") can be treated as animals, or worse. It's not just that those born into the lower castes are materially poor— it is that they are *supposed to be poor*. This is their lot in life.

THE FACES OF POVERTY

Sometimes, looking into the eyes of Indian villagers, I can feel the lost sadness of their hearts. I see these lost souls sitting in the dirt outside their primitive dwellings, which typically are stick, thatch, and mud huts, staring silently forward. For them there are no dreams of advancement, no vision of a better life ahead, no opportunities to improve things for their children. Theirs is a life of depressed endurance—struggling to have enough to eat, bearing the insults of society, paying for supposed evils committed in past lives.

Sometimes their stares remain unbroken, even when I (a strange sight to behold in an Indian village) walk by. But I've learned something interesting about Indian culture. Everyone from the youngest child playing in the field to the oldest, most wrinkled, sunbaked woman on the street responds to the traditional Indian greeting. You've probably seen it. Hands together in front of your chest, as if in a stance of prayer, a smile, and then a slight bow. The most skeptical, sullen, or sad-faced individuals reciprocate the greeting, usually smiling, but at minimum bobbing their heads from side to side in approval. Even though no words are exchanged, this greeting can break through an empty stare and establish a connection.

One such woman was sitting quietly outside a pastel-painted building in Salem as the visiting team of U.S. pastors I was part of disembarked from a bus one Sunday morning to walk to a church meeting. I glanced at the woman, who was staring at us with absolutely no expression on her face. We were all about to pass by when I felt prompted by the Holy Spirit to greet her. The moment she saw my greeting, her head bobbled from side to side. She smiled and returned the greeting.

A few moments later, our group arrived at the church and went in to join a worship service already in progress. Not long after, I noticed the woman come in the rear of the cinder block sanctuary, remove her sandals, and sit in the very back on the floor. Since most village churches have no chairs, it is customary for those who have shoes to remove them before being seated "Indian style" on the floor. After the service, I learned it was this woman's first time to attend the church, and the pastor's wife was going to take a few moments to share the gospel with her.

I like to think that my simple greeting, acknowledging her especially out of the throngs of people we passed by on our way to church that day, made a difference in her life. She is the epitome of how I would describe so many souls in India—lost eyes, but open hearts. They hunger for the same things you and I do. They need the love of God to fill the emptiness of their hearts. They need a sense of worth and a vision. But idolatry, poverty, and the cyclical, hopeless assumptions about life's purpose built into lower caste culture offer nothing but continuing despair and an inner sense of sadness.

THE HOPE OF CHRIST

Jesus can change all of that in an instant! In Christ, a person can experience purpose, individual value, forgiveness of sins, and an eternal hope that far outweighs even the worst suffering in this world. Imagine what it means to a lower caste Hindu (who lives in fear of the local spirits behind family idols) to hear the gospel. To learn what the apostle Paul wrote to the Romans, "You did not receive the spirit of slavery to fall back into fear, but you have been received by the Spirit of adoption as sons, by whom we cry, 'Abba! Father!'" (Romans 8:15). Or to hear Paul's words, "I consider that the sufferings of this present time are not worth comparing with the glory that is to be revealed in us" (Romans 8:18). "What then shall we say to these things? If God is for us, who can be against us? . . . Who shall separate us from the love of Christ?" (Romans 8:31-35).

Of course, people in the upper castes need Jesus as well, in the same way all of us do. They are at the top of the growing

Asian economy, with lifestyles and amenities that can make a trip for you or me to an Indian city increasingly feel like home. Yes, the occasional ox cart still ambles along the streets with busses, cars, motorcycles, and bicycles in a dizzying tangle of activity. And dogs, cows, and even sheep are not uncommon in the streets of the smaller cities. Beggars are everywhere, all the time, every age. But upper caste people live in luxury, many in lifestyles equivalent to or higher than average Westerners. Most large cities have established churches as well as ongoing missionary efforts, such as the work of the Salvation Army, that provide ongoing evangelization and compassion ministries. (This is not to imply that the cities of India have been "reached" with the gospel, but residents of cities might at least find occasional access to the Christian message.)

But what we can see in Mumbai or New Delhi, as massive as those cities have grown, is only a sliver of Indian life. Most people—seventy percent, in fact—live in villages that are only now beginning to enjoy some technological advances that much of the world has enjoyed for over a century. They are the ones most in need of hearing and receiving the hope of Christ.

THE CHALLENGE

Stepping into the unreached villages of India for Westerners is like stepping backwards in time hundreds of years. In a larger village you would find a public square filled with vendors and merchants. You would see a Hindu temple, filled with idols and adorned with colorful flowers and paintings. Electric wires (definitely not "up to code") would likely be strung between thatch roof dwellings and sheet metal homes. In contrast, smaller villages typically are so poor they lack all of these amenities and are merely a grouping of earthen huts surrounded by hand-tended farm fields, with a small shrine at some place of honor in the area.

Millions of Indians live and die in such villages, knowing little of the outside world. An average Indian woman treks to a community well to draw water for her family every day, often passing by open sewers and piles of smoldering trash along her dusty way. Sometimes a small library and grade school is present, the result of an initiative by a local government official or non-profit agency. Little exists beyond those resources, so literacy and connectedness to the larger world are rare.

What did Jesus mean when He said He was anointed to preach the good news to the poor? What does His anointing have to do with us? Who can accept the challenge of carrying the gospel to these places, so foreign to you and me?

More than half of the 600,000 village communities in India still lack a gospel witness. Many villagers wouldn't recognize the name of Jesus. Others may have a cultural or historical understanding of Christianity but know nothing about the personal relationship with Jesus Christ that is possible through the gospel. And how would they? Without the wealth to afford transportation and without modern communications, how would they hear the gospel unless someone went to their village, shared the gospel, and helped them plant a church?

It is hard to imagine the sheer volume of need in South Asia, let alone the rest of the globe. It is easy to be moved to tears by the physical plight of so many millions of people living without clean water, adequate education, or medical care in such poverty as to defy description. But even more heartbreaking, in reality, is to look into the eyes of people who have never heard of a God who loves them, who have no church in their village, and thus have little hope of access to the kingdom of God. Their eternal fate is far worse than their earthly one. They are, as the Bible explains, "having no hope and without God in the world" (Ephesians 2:12).

This hopelessness is reversed when Jesus Christ is introduced.

THE APPROACH

One of the foundational principles of India Gospel League and the Vision 2000 movement is to lead with the gospel, not with humanitarian aid. Many mission groups approach their efforts the other way around, and they have their reasons for doing so. But India Gospel League knows by experience that the blessings of the gospel cannot flow in any sustainable or truly helpful way without an "outpost" of God's kingdom—a local church planted in a region of need. The gospel *always* goes first; then, if possible, education, medical care, job training, clean water wells, and more.

India Gospel League encourages self-sustainability as early as possible in newly planted churches. Rather than receiving handouts from an outside group that is "here today, gone tomorrow," villagers instead receive aid through their own local church—the "hands and feet" of Jesus in their village—without any outside assistance. In other situations, IGL connects the dots between a village church and a partner congregation (either another in India or a church group in another country) to assist in the provision of help to those most in need, be they the sick, orphaned, widows, illiterate, or in many cases, the entire village.

If you were to ask Rev. Stephens today what the greatest need in India was, he wouldn't say education or government reform or even job opportunities for the poor. He would say, without apology, that the need is *Jesus*. The need is the heart change Christ can bring that results in the life change people so desperately need. It is Jesus who frees the captives. It is Jesus who brings good news to the poor. It is Jesus who transforms human beings into the glorious children of God they were always intended to be. Start with Jesus, lead with the gospel, and then watch as His power changes everything else.

It doesn't take long when visiting rural India to recognize how destructive the caste system and the related idol worship of Hinduism is to human potential. Many people give the best of all they have in the ritual worship of idols, gain nothing in return, and still trudge on, believing themselves to be worthless or under some form of ancient judgment. But in the midst of this despair, there is one place where caste has *no meaning*. There is one gathering where "all men are created equal" and everyone can live, laugh, sing, learn, and pray. *That place is the Christian church.* And that's just one reason why church planting is critical to meeting both the spiritual and the physical needs of South Asia. Without Christianity, without a renewal of purpose and a restoration to the dignity God created every person to embody, humanitarian help is a mere temporary comfort in a life otherwise defined by darkness.

The cultural situation for Christians in India isn't that different from the world where the gospel was first introduced. In the Bible there was plenty of tension between Jews and Gentiles, Greeks and Romans, locals and foreigners, slaves and free. All those cultures amalgamated by the Roman Empire were forced to live together, some with more rights than others. Yet into this broken cultural context, the early church was born.

To the church at Colossae, Paul wrote, "Here there is not Greek and Jew, circumcised and uncircumcised, barbarian, Scythian, slave, free; but Christ is all, and in all" (Colossians 3:11). Perhaps for our purposes we could add a few other designations to this verse: "Here, in the Christian church, it also doesn't matter if you are American or Indian, from Tamil Nadu or from Tampa Bay, Eastern, Western, Dalit, Brahmin, poor, or prosperous; Christ is everything!"

THE CALLED

The Great Commission in South Asia is being advanced, in large part, by "average" men and women called and committed to the cause. The faithful "barefoot pastors" travel to villages, some beyond where all the roads end, to set Christ before the lost eyes of multitudes. They are on the front lines of reaching the unreached, the untouched, the unloved. They give up everything, some even their lives, to serve the Great Commission. Ordinary people? Yes, but with extraordinary desire to serve God.

I recall one man sitting cross-legged on the stone floor of a village church in central India, singing and praising with all of his might. When an opportunity for public testimony was presented, he stated with humble excitement that he wanted to carry the gospel to a village that had never heard of Jesus before. After the meeting, Sam Stephens turned to me and asked a rhetorical question that I'll never forget. "What's making him say that? What is causing that man to have such a drive to share the gospel?"

Obviously we know who is behind that desire. *The Holy Spirit* is empowering God's servants to go and make disciples. He is giving these humble servants a vision to carry on the Great Commission work in this generation. He's leading men and women to forsake everything familiar and follow Jesus.

Some will face persecution for their decision. Some will leave their homes. Some will be disowned by their parents. Some will face obstacles that, humanly speaking, are insurmountable. And yet they go. They obey. They share.

And me? You? Well, *we have the same power.* And the Holy Spirit is putting the same desire in our hearts as that man in the arid mountains of midwest India has in his. It is time to share the Messiah with our world. With our generation. In every city, in every village, to every language, to every nation. It is time to *lead* with the gospel. In our world are billions of lost eyes, and thanks to God's grace, multitudes of open hearts.

All they need is a messenger.

DISCUSS IT

Describe a time the Holy Spirit prompted you to share the gospel with someone. What happened?

Sometimes, an opportunity to share Christ begins with a simple greeting or extension of friendship. In what ways could you "greet" the world around you?

What is your initial reaction to IGL's approach to always "lead with the gospel"?

When you hear about the devotion of Indian Christians, do you think it would be easier or harder for average people in our country to make such a commitment to the gospel?

ACT ON IT

This week, make a point to greet the people you pass by. Your choice of action could be as simple as eye contact and a smile, a wave, or even a verbal greeting or friendly question. Perhaps God will soon put you in the path of someone who is desperate for encouragement or who needs to hear the gospel.

SHARE IT

I believe in Jesus Christ because . . .

A South Indian woman with her child, one of thousands who have access to the gospel today because a church planter came to her region about ten years ago.

Idols and sacred stones near a rural village. Millions of individual gods and goddesses are worshipped and feared in the Hindu regions of India.

As the gospel spreads, so does the joy of knowing Jesus personally.

CHAPTER 4

THE HARVEST IS PLENTIFUL

Sometimes God calls us to answer our own prayers.

When Jesus sent seventy-two of His followers out to announce His arrival to the villages He was about to enter, He said, "The harvest is plentiful, but the laborers are few. Therefore pray earnestly to the Lord of the harvest to send out laborers into his harvest. Go your way . . ." (Luke 10:2-3).

I love that two-step directive from Jesus: "Pray for more workers! Now (you) go!"

Oops. Lord, I prayed for more workers. *Other* workers. Not *me*!

If you've felt that way, you're in good company. Tongue-tied Moses didn't think he was qualified. Cowardly Gideon wondered if the angel was crazy for calling him "mighty warrior." The apostle Paul wrote of "weakness and much trembling" as he would preach the gospel.

Yet in God's power they stood. They fought. They preached. And through them, God changed history.

When Jesus entered a Samaritan village, as recorded in John 4, He broke two cultural taboos. First, He spoke to a woman. Even worse, she was a *Samaritan* woman. Upon returning from their hunt for food, the disciples were shocked to see their Master with her. They didn't realize Jesus had just shared the message of living water with a very thirsty soul. They were thinking about filling their bellies, but Jesus was thinking about the grand mission God had Him on earth to accomplish. That's when He explained, "My food is to do the will of him who sent me and to accomplish his work. Do you not say, 'There are yet four months, then comes the harvest?' Look, I tell you, lift up your eyes, and see that the fields are white for harvest."

Many Samaritans believed in Jesus based on the testimony of the woman. They came out to meet Christ and asked Him to stay and share more. After two days, the rest of the village community said to the woman, "It is no longer because of what you said that we believe, for we have heard for ourselves, and we know that this is indeed the Savior of the world" (John 4:1-42).

Often we get the idea that the "harvest isn't ready"—that people won't listen, that other cultures are more open to the gospel than our own, or that somehow we just shouldn't expect such results. And there's a kernel of truth in that. Some people really do harden their hearts against God's Word. But get the picture here: The disciples would have said that about the Samaritans. They weren't "close" to God at all (in the Jewish mindset). They were hard-hearted, compromised sinners who would be the last to accept the Messiah.

Yet Jesus called His followers to view the world differently: *Wake up and look around! The fields are ripe! The harvest is ready!*

And it was. The whole village turned to Christ!

A "SAMARITAN" VILLAGE IN INDIA

I don't think I'd ever had a real mental picture of what that Samaritan village looked like until I walked into a hillside community in Maharashtra. As our traveling team approached, it suddenly clicked in my head: "This village probably looks similar to the ones Jesus visited. This community, this way of living, this laid-back country lifestyle without any electronics—this is the stuff of the Gospels and the book of Acts. I'm in it!"

The setting, the feeling, the sights, the smells, the ox carts, the farmers tending to their fields by hand, the total silence, the absence of wires and towers and planes—this is rural, classic India. Our bus had brought us as close as possible, about two kilometers away. We hiked the rest up a narrow, dusty, uphill trail before we entered this town consisting of mud huts with thatched roofs, a few communal areas, and half-naked children.

Could places like this be ready for the gospel, even though for centuries they'd worshipped idols, having never heard of Christianity?

Here's the answer: In this particular village, twenty-five percent of the population had turned to Christ in about four years. (Imagine that happening in your city!)

I wish you could see what I saw—that you too could interview the men and women who make villages like this one their mission field. They often come to situations like this without any material support—just a vision to serve Jesus.

In this particular village, the pastor and his wife lived in a small stone structure attached to a tiny church building, their living quarters no larger than a small bedroom, by North American standards. They greeted us with beaming smiles, couldn't wait to report on the great things God had done, and were proud to share with us some of their spicy rice! I can't imagine the trials, frustrations, discouragements, and needs of this church planter and his family; but here they were, on a remote hillside, faithfully advancing the kingdom of Christ.

When God puts people with bold faith into remote rural villages that serve idols (really, the spirits represented by the painted wood and clay figurines), explosive things start to happen. This shouldn't surprise us in the least.

After all, what happened when Jesus walked into a village? What happened when Paul and Silas entered a new city? Everything from demon manifestations to healing miracles, angry crowds to mass conversions!

The same is true for unreached India. Introduce the light, and the powers of darkness strike back. Preach about the power of Jesus, and be prepared for Him to demonstrate it.

LABORERS FOR THE GOSPEL

The one thing a ripe harvest needs is workers. That's why Jesus told His disciples to pray, not necessarily for open hearts or willing converts, but simply for *laborers*. The harvest is sitting there in the field. The need is not for more souls to save, but for people to go forth with the gospel and reach out to them.

In South Asia the need is great, possibly greater than in any other region of the world. We need thousands of pastors, Bible study leaders, orphan foster parents, medical workers, and joyful servants willing to offer themselves and whatever skills they have to share Christ and all the love He has to offer.

The amazing thing is that many of these laborers are already there—already speaking the language, already willing to go forth—but they haven't been sent. They haven't been resourced or trained. Many of them go anyway, with or without means for support, trusting God for provision.

INDIGENOUS AND SELF-SUSTAINING

When Jesus sent His disciples out to preach the gospel, He told them to go first to the neighboring areas and then beyond. Further, He told them to find a way to support themselves by connecting with the people wherever they went. What can we learn about these principles as we consider how to fulfill the Great Commission in this generation?

India Gospel League can teach us. It operates with what mission agencies call an *indigenous* and *self-sustaining* approach. Simply put, this means that the workers sent out are those God has already raised up within a given people group, whenever possible. It also means that these workers must establish a way to support themselves within a short period of time so the ministry they plant is not dependent on outside help.

A native church planter already knows the local culture and lives according to local customs. A foreign missionary might require many thousands of dollars for language training, travel, and ongoing living expenses, but a native worker may require only a few hundred dollars for training and start-up. For example, as of 2014, a "barefoot pastor" commissioned through India Gospel League can labor full time for about $100 USD per month. He is expected to establish himself in a village as well as establish a church there.

But more than the fact that this approach to missions is less costly and more flexible, there is deeper reason to encourage indigenous church planting and leadership whenever possible. In the long term, the church that grows and reaches out to its neighbors to establish more churches must be *local*, not foreign. In the chapters to come, we will explore more about why this approach is the best way forward for missions in South Asia (and really, everywhere).

I recently asked Sam Stephens about the greatest need India Gospel League faces going forward. He said without hesitation, "More barefoot pastors to be supported on a temporary basis." They are willing to join the Vision 2000 movement, willing to go where no Christians have gone before, willing to invest themselves in planting churches . . . but they need to be sent. They need that initial jump-start into ministry!

To join the Vision 2000 movement today, pastors and church planters must commit to seek out unreached village areas and plant a new church group *every year.* India Gospel League, through its supporting partners, assists pastors with their expenses for the first two of those years. After that time, it is expected that the churches they've planted will provide ongoing support for them as they identify and train leaders to replace them. They then move on to the next area (just like the apostle Paul did in the first century).

Now, many people in India speak some English, since not that long ago, their land was a part of the British Empire. In fact, most signage in India is in both English and one of the fourteen major regional languages. It is not uncommon for Indian citizens to use English to communicate with each other when they are from different areas of their country. So, occasionally in my interviews, I was able to carry on conversations without a translator. I encountered a short, cheerful Indian man who spoke great English, and I used the opportunity to dive a little deeper into his thinking and vision.

This man had planted seven churches since he began his ministry in the Vision 2000 movement. He told me that he would ride his bike between these seven churches each week, holding one church meeting each morning, and spending the rest of the afternoon caring for needs in that given village. Imagine running seven churches, one for every day of the week! But my friend wasn't content with what he had done so far. He told me he and his trainee had identified an eighth unreached village in their vicinity, and they had begun evangelistic efforts there.

How small my vision has been! Eight churches? Eight villages? One pastor? A bicycle? When I asked him about his long-range plan, he replied with a broad smile: "I am praying that the Lord allows me to see one thousand churches planted before I die!"

Such are the barefoot pastors of India. It is rare to meet one who shepherds only one flock. Most have branch churches in nearby villages; most have initiated leadership training to reproduce their ministry into the lives of younger pastors. And on top of their preaching, evangelism, and prayer and care for the sick, many end up adopting needy children or initiating various help ministries for the very poor.

The IGL team is praying to send hundreds of additional laborers into the remaining areas of India that have no gospel witness. And with believers who harbor such vision for Christ's kingdom, it is no surprise the India Gospel League's outreach is growing rapidly. It is no surprise that now, after centuries of darkness, India is being reached exponentially with the gospel.

Paul wrote to the early Roman church about the need for mission focus:

> For everyone who calls on the name of the Lord will
> be saved. How then will they call on him in whom
> they have not believed? And how are they to believe
> in him of whom they have never heard? And how

are they to hear without someone preaching? And how are they to preach unless they are sent? As it is written, "How beautiful are the feet of those who preach the good news!" (Romans 10:13-15).

In India today, men, women, and children are hearing the gospel for the first time. Hundreds of thousands are entering the kingdom of God. Yet the work isn't over. Still millions cannot call upon Him because they have never heard of Him. And they won't hear unless someone is sent to tell them!

India Gospel League is actively training and recruiting men and women to carry the message, to hold forth the Word of life. And, with whatever resources they have, they are sending these laborers into God's great Asian harvest. More could be done, of course. More must be done. The most populous and least-reached region on the planet is, in this moment, open for the gospel. The harvest is plentiful.

Of course, the harvest near you is plentiful as well. From Delhi to Denmark to Denver, there are souls in need—men, women, and children—who face both earthly and eternal questions that only Jesus Christ can answer. Our "Samaritan village" is just past the region we are comfortable reaching— an area on the other side of town, a village on the other side of a mountain, or a country on the other side of the world.

Will you pray for laborers in the great harvest? Will you go to your Samaritan village?

DISCUSS IT

What are your thoughts about the extent to which the world around you is open or closed to hearing about the gospel? Is the problem with the fields or with the workers? Why?

The Vision 2000 movement sometimes offers two years of support for their pastors. Why do you think this two-year window is important? Why not continue supporting the pastors indefinitely?

To what extent do you consider yourself a worker in the harvest field? How would you describe a next step for you, and what would you need in the way of support to take it?

ACT ON IT

If you are unsure of how to best reach out to your own community, set up a meeting with a group of friends who love Jesus and want to share Him with the world. Begin praying together about what you can do, as a group, to reach out.

SHARE IT

The first time I heard about #Christianity, I was . . .

Farmers in India often live on the equivalent of just a few dollars a day; village economies have been based on simple farming methods for centuries.

Boys from one of IGL's children's homes excited to meet a foreigner. Plenty of smiles and laughs!

Passionate prayer is one of the defining characteristics of Indian churches.

Pastors from the IGL church planting network gather at a pastors' conference for training and fellowship.

CHAPTER 5

GROWING KINGDOM LEADERS

Jesus spent a great portion of His three ministry years (before His death and resurrection) growing His disciples into kingdom leaders. He knew the Commission He would soon give them would require strong leadership, humble attitudes, and bold vision. For all of this, Jesus knew they needed divine training.

In South Asia, many believers become pastors out of necessity, without any formal theological training, because the need is so great. After all, if an excited new believer ventures to an unreached community, shares the gospel, and people start to respond, who must function as the pastor? These faithful servants simply share what they know and learn as they go.

A key strategic objective for the church in this region of the world is to provide *depth* that corresponds with its rapidly expanding *breadth*. Doing so involves identifying these pastor-leaders, training them, and encouraging them to stay true to God's Word.

One my favorite people in India has to be Pastor Benjamin (affectionately known by most as "Benny"), the man charged with coordinating leadership training for India Gospel League. His mission is to bring the thousands of church leaders who are part of Vision 2000 into contexts where they can be encouraged, built up, offered doctrinal and practical education, and sent back out with renewed passion for the gospel.

Pastor Benny crisscrosses India on a regular basis, often with Sam Stephens, to bring village pastors together for two-day conferences, weeklong trainings, and leadership retreats. When foreign pastors (like me) and other Christian leaders are invited to come to India, they are asked to serve as guest speakers in such meetings.

Benny's story reveals more about why this broad movement is happening now and what IGL's assumptions are moving forward. Here's what he shared with me.

> In the 1980s, when I was being trained for ministry, we were always told we should "tell the gospel to someone!" Direct evangelism was the highest value. We formed teams and showed up in villages to share Christ. We'd preach open-air, sing songs, show *The JESUS Film*, and hand out literature. Then the people would go home, and so would we.
>
> The gospel was being proclaimed, but the people weren't being *discipled*. And how could they be? There was no church in their village!

We partnered with groups such as Campus Crusade (known today as Cru) for materials and media. Pastors would come to IGL to get these resources and then take them out to more villages. But what was the next step?

Then, in the early 90s, Sam Stephens asked an important question: "We are only doing the first part of the Great Commission; why we aren't fulfilling it? The gospel is going out, but disciples aren't being made."

That's when Vision 2000 started to form. "We will ask our traveling evangelists to stay in a village for at least twelve months, to train the believers and establish a permanent church," Sam explained. "We will ask them to select a village where there is no church, and to start one. And not only this year, but *every* year."

This was the first time we really started teaching the rest of the Great Commission—not only sharing the gospel, but also *teaching people to obey all that Jesus commanded* (Matthew 28:19-20). We had determined that only by planting a permanent church could God's kingdom really be established in a given village.

We themed our next training conference around church planting and master planning strategies to help the barefoot pastors learn how to begin churches and organize their work. Then we invited them to gather every quarter for prayer and training. But soon this became difficult, since India Gospel League's outreach was spreading out more and more. So we encouraged the pastors to meet in their own regions and appoint regional leaders, and periodically we would come to them to provide ongoing training. We are trying to pattern this approach after the book of Acts model with Paul and Barnabas.

FLEXIBLE METHODOLOGY

One feature of IGL's Great Commission strategy that strikes me is how flexible it is. Movements are always flexible, not necessarily in their doctrine or their mission, but in their methodology. India Gospel League allows each pastor in each region to approach the unique needs of his own village. Sam and Benny recommend some common "blueprints" for how churches are planted, but they also leave plenty of room for the Holy Spirit to direct.

With rapt attention, I listened to the rest of Benny's story.

First, the pastor or I or someone from India Gospel League approaches the headman of a village, asking his permission to come into the village for the purpose of establishing a church. After permission is obtained, the pastor and his family, if he has one, move to the village and begin building friendships and doing direct evangelism. The approach might be as simple as saying, "Hello, I am a Christian pastor, and I am beginning a church in your village. Have you ever heard of Christ?"

Some of our workers will do this kind of seed-planting work in multiple villages at the same time. Very often God miraculously answers a prayer for someone who is sick, addicted, or demon possessed in order to show His power over the spirits the people have been worshipping. As men, women, and children begin putting their faith in Jesus, small group Bible studies and Children's Gospel Clubs (like Vacation Bible School in the U.S.) are formed.

Once there are twenty or more baptized adult believers meeting together weekly, the group is considered to be a church." In most situations, after the two-year startup period, the pastor is able to be supported by his newly planted church, and the work becomes self-sustaining. On average, a Vision 2000 pastor will continue his commitment to plant one new church every year for several years, which also compels him to train additional leaders to carry the work forward. The whole orientation of village churches is toward multiplying the gospel work, serving the needy, and training up biblical leaders.

I needed one more answer from Benny. "Okay, in the U.S we would also encourage a church to plant another congregation or launch a multi-site campus, but usually we wait until our base church is really healthy and established. If we said, 'Let's start a new work every year,' in our context, people would look at us like we were crazy. Why don't you allow village churches time to grow some roots before they start multiplying?"

Benny replied quickly with a smile, "Does a farmer only plant one seed and then wait for it to grow?"

LIFE CENTERS

Based on the economic situation in the village, many churches in India are unable to afford buildings of any kind. New believers meet first in homes. Later, if possible, they build simple, open-air, stick and thatch structures they call "prayer huts." The availability of land is a major hurdle for any structure in which to meet. Land must be donated or purchased by someone in the village.

When it is time, and if funds become available, the pastor and the village believers develop a plan for the next step: a permanent Life Center. It is a simple stone building concept that serves as a worship center as well as a place where education, community development, skills training, fresh water from a new well, and child care can be provided. Most of the life centers I saw in India were only slightly larger than a one-car garage.

Even as this development takes place, India Gospel League takes great care to ensure that the young local church does not become dependent on outside help (be it from other churches in India or from foreign supporters). Funding to build always requires an investment by the village church-goers themselves, and, if additional help is required, it must be only temporary. For example, the economy of the village might be so small that building a church or providing job training to residents would be impossible without partial assistance at the beginning.

In cases such as this, India Gospel League looks to its ongoing partnerships with churches, businesses, and individuals elsewhere in the world who are willing to come alongside a village pastor and help jump-start the work with funds ($8,000 on average) for building materials. Of course, the villagers themselves must build the building.

EARLY CHURCH ISSUES

While I had Benny's attention, I thought I'd ask him a few questions about the spiritual life of the men and women leaders who serve. Being on the front lines of spiritual warfare must come with some risks, difficulties, and temptations. What about divisions in the infant churches? What about converts who slip back into idolatry? What about the poverty and the continual lack of resources? And this on top of the opposition from other religious groups that are unhappy about the church's presence? Benny explained:

> We get discouraged or tired sometimes. In those moments we need to slow down. I really appreciate when God brings me a story of how He used me to help someone, and that gives me renewed motivation to continue with my work. For example, I was sharing with a group of pastors yesterday, and afterward I went to dinner with one family. The pastor told me, "I was struggling in our church, and I was thinking about how discouraged I've been for the last three months. But this afternoon, God spoke to me through your words, Pastor Benny." Moments like that help me remember to keep going, *that I have to keep going.* I also receive a lot of comfort when I read God's Word.

As for temptations, they are all around us, wherever we go. God helps me through the accountability and stories I receive from other pastors. It helps that we are always working as a team. We need each other. When I am down, I have someone to help me and lift me up. I never would say I have enough strength by myself.

These words remind me a lot of Paul's encouragements to the New Testament churches in his letters. Like in 1 and 2 Timothy, when Paul mentions his co-workers, or offers some word of specific encouragement to a church at the end of a letter. To a Christian worker on the front lines, statements like, "Grace and peace to you from God our Father and the Lord Jesus Christ" and "Grace to all of you who love our Lord Jesus with an undying love" are more than friendly reminders. God's grace and peace are the lifelines they hold onto in the midst of humanly insurmountable challenges!

So much of what's happening in rural India reminds me of Bible times—from the culture to the growth of the church, from the spiritual opposition to the mentoring of leaders. In a way, Sam Stephens and Pastor Benny function as apostles for these young Indian churches.

I doubt they'd use such terminology to describe themselves, but that's what I see. I see Sam and Benny (and others you are going to hear about in the next few chapters) sharing, serving, loving, and training. They are traveling to encourage fledgling churches, helping local leaders develop vision to reach into new areas, praying with those most in need, writing letters of instruction and encouragement, and networking hundreds of leaders to share the gospel vision for South Asia.

I'm used to saying, "Back in Bible times, such-and-such happened," when I preach or teach or write. When I am in India, I see those New Testament church issues being lived out in present-day reality. Maybe, by making the connection, you and I can live in "Bible times" after all!

WHERE DO WE START?

Pastor Benny shared his heart motivations regarding the Great Commission and what he recommends for people like you and me who want to get started in a new way on the Great Commission task.

> The first thing is to surrender your whole life to God. It's not, "What can I do for God?" It's, "What can God do through me?" Open your heart to what God wants to teach, what He wants to do.

> Sometimes we are like Moses. We say to God, "I'm ineligible. I can't do it. Lord, there must be another way." At other times, we are like Jonah. We receive the call from God, but we'd rather do something different.

> My own story is like this. I wanted to be a church planter in a specific region of India, but God directed me to my current position. I had to finally say "yes" to God's call for me.

Following, living for, and sharing Christ—this is the definition of the Christian life. If you don't do those things, you aren't a Christian. You need to read His Word and really consider what He is commanding you to do. In India, we encourage believers to share the gospel with at least one other person before they request to be baptized. Doing so helps them grow in their faith and be strengthened. Only after they have shared the gospel are they qualified to make a public testimony through baptism.

Practically, here's what I'd recommend. Find some non-Christian friends and start praying for them. Take on the goal to share the gospel personally with at least one person every twelve months. As you pray for a non-Christian, contact him, share the gospel, befriend him, and spend time with him so that you can lead him to Christ.

But remember, we cannot spread God's kingdom by ourselves. We need the presence of God, the guidance of the Holy Spirit. Before we share, the Holy Spirit has to prepare us and prepare the heart of our listener. I have talked with people who think sharing the gospel is a special gift. But it isn't a unique gift. *It is a gift every follower of Christ has when the Holy Spirit comes inside you.* It is the nature of every Christian, because of the Holy Spirit, to be salt and light.

That is the reason God created me. That is the reason God has chosen me. In the past He prepared me step by step for this time in my life. Since I was fourteen years old, I knew He wanted me to be involved in missions. In this generation, for this generation, I am in India. It is a great opportunity and a great privilege to be part of fulfilling the Great Commission. That is why I am here. I have no other reason.

What's your reason for being where you are, doing what you do? What's mine? Have we set our hearts on the completion of the Great Commission in our generation? In our city, in our country? Across the planet? With our co-workers, our neighborhood, our own family? With the time God gives us? With the money He entrusts to us? With the remaining years of life we have?

God is looking for surrendered, obedient hearts that will simply say, "Yes." *Yes, I'll go. Yes, I'll take risks. Yes, Jesus, I'll obey.*

DISCUSS IT

How do you think the commitment to annual church multiplication impacts the ministry of a pastor and the mentality of a congregation?

Pastor Benny has a defined sense of purpose from God regarding his life. How do you define your sense of purpose? How is it like his and different from his?

One role that teamwork plays in Pastor Benny's ministry is to keep him strong against temptation and discouragement. In your Christian life, who is on your team? How could you strengthen that bond?

ACT ON IT

Pastor Benny recommends that we select one non-Christian to personally impact. In your life, who could this be? Put that individual's initials in a place where you will be reminded to pray for him/her daily, and begin looking for opportunities to serve, love, and share the gospel with that person.

SHARE IT

#Praying for friends is important to me. Is there any way I could pray for you?

Every year, thousands of women are trained to lead Bible studies, transformation groups, and community service projects.

Heroes of faith—men who pray and work hard to reach those without Christ.

IGL offers leadership conferences to men, women, and youth who wish to carry the gospel forward. For many, these meetings are their only opportunity for training.

Pastor Raja sharing from the Scriptures in preparation to baptize three new believers.

CHAPTER 6

BOLD WITNESSES

I n a nation as vast and varied as India, there is no shortage of people to meet. But some people, even though you can't speak their language, live in your memory and in your heart. The church-planting pastors I've met along the way have been like that. Each one of them probably deserves a biography all their own. Here I'll share just a few stories to give you an idea of what it's like to walk the road of a barefoot pastor—the kind of faith required, the miraculous fruit that results. My prayer is that these bold witnesses will inspire you to join God in His work in your world.

PASTOR BENJAMIN—ATHEIST NO MORE

Benjamin was born in a Hindu family, but he had his doubts. His father was an alcoholic, and life was difficult. As Benjamin grew up, he was increasingly hostile to spiritual things. Eventually he joined a group of atheists and went around the region proclaiming, "There are no gods!"

Soon, he became the group's leader. Though he had no peace or joy in his life, he was convinced that God, the gods, and spiritual things were all contrived. Then something happened that would change him forever.

> One day I became very sick, so bad that my throat and really my whole body had symptoms. A local hospital tested me and told my mother, "We cannot treat your son. Only God can heal him."

> My mother appealed to me. "Maybe if you believe in God, He can heal you! The God's name is Jesus."

> So I did actually pray something. I said, "If there is a God, let Him heal me."

> My mother brought in a pastor, who said, "Jesus is God, He died for you, and He will give you life."

> And you know, in that moment, I was healed! I accepted Jesus Christ right then and determined to do God's ministry from then on. Since that day, I have planted five churches.

PASTOR JOHN—HUMBLE TESTIMONY

Pastor John has worked with India Gospel League for twenty-five years, since the beginning of the Vision 2000 movement. He is humble and soft-spoken, but his story is just one more showcase of the hard, prayerful work Indian men and women are doing for the sake of the gospel.

I was born into a nominally Christian family and ended up working in a coal mine. I thought I was a Christian, but I really wasn't following God. I had no relationship with Him.

Once, at my job site, I fell into a pool of water. Since I didn't know how to swim, I was in real danger. I cried out, "God, save my life!" I was rescued, and that near-death incident caused me to rethink everything.

My co-workers were amazed, saying, "You know, only God could save you from that situation." So I accepted Jesus as my personal Savior and began living for Him. It wasn't long before I heard the call of God to join the ministry. I went to seminary for two years, and then, in the late 1980s, I met Sam Stephens and joined India Gospel League.

I have planted five churches, thousands of Hindus have heard the gospel, and right now I am starting a new work in an additional village. Things started to pick up in this new village when one woman accepted Jesus. She started a prayer group, and soon her husband also became a Christian. From there we started a new congregation that has been reaching out to the needy in our area. Recently a woman who had cancer was miraculously healed, and that has opened another door for us to share about Jesus.

ANNIE—HAPPY TO DO GOD'S WORK

Women play a key role in reaching lost souls in the villages of India, and through IGL's Women with a Mission (WWM) movement, they are reaching village women by the thousands. The WWM workers start Bible studies, and they also provide skills training for village women—nursing care, hygiene training, and rural development expertise—all desperately needed services. Here is Annie's story:

When I was in seventh grade, I accepted the Lord Jesus Christ. I was staying in a mission because I had no father or mother. When I finished my study, I thought it would be good to not get married, just to work for God for my whole life. So I started teaching, singing, and helping children.

I had a friend who talked to me about IGL and Vision 2000, and I thought, "What is this? This is not good for me. I am already trained. I am already in ministry." But after prayer, I decided to learn more. Since then I have been able to offer many of IGL's materials in my ministry, leading Children's Gospel Clubs, teaching Sunday school, and more. I attend the regional trainings offered by Vision 2000, and this helps me very much. I am very happy to do God's work.

In partnership with The Gideons International, we are giving away free Bibles and trying to educate as many as we can. More than 2,000 girls have come through our orphan and children's home. Now many of these are getting married and taking their Bibles with them!

PASTOR KUMAR—HOMELESS AND RICH

Pastor Kumar is one of those magnetic personalities that lights up a room upon entry. His white hair and compelling smile exude wisdom mixed with good cheer. He too had joined with IGL in the early days, and he too captured the vision for church multiplication across India. He was also a part of the 2004 tsunami relief efforts along the coast. He jumped at the chance to speak about all that God has done in his ministry. Though a translator was available, he looked right at me and said, "Can you understand my non-gramm-atic-al English?"

I started with a simple question. "How has God been working in your village?"

> There have been healings recently, including a man who was going to have his leg amputated due to leprosy. I asked to pray for him, and he was completely healed.
>
> Another lady was healed from cancer. We have story after story. But there is more to it than that. The area where I am working now has been known as a place of murderers and thieves and other wicked people. People from surrounding villages would not come to ours. But since the gospel has been introduced, their lifestyle has slowly been changing. In fact, the regional government noticed this and has since offered assistance. Many members of my church used to be alcoholics, gang members, and murderers!

Then, as if worried that our interview might end, he said, "And, Sir, wait, could I share with you my testimony?" I gladly agreed.

I was born in 1952. When I was a five months old, my mother died. I lived like an orphan during my childhood; no one cared for me. My step-mother fed me, but there was no love. After school I started spending time with bad friends, and they led me the wrong way. I lost all hope for my life and attempted suicide two times. God directly saved me—I tried to jump off a mountain, and a hand grabbed me!

In 1970 someone handed me a New Testament, and I learned about Jesus. I did not accept Him immediately, because in my childhood I was an idol worshipper. But I was curious to learn more. So I compared the Christian Bible, the Hindu holy texts, and also a Muslim Koran. I read all three, and it became obvious to me that Jesus Christ is the Lord I should worship. I enrolled at a Bible seminary so that I could serve Jesus.

In 1973 I was fasting, and God spoke to me through Hebrews 11:8 and Genesis 12:2, that I should get up and go to an unknown place. "But God, where will I go?" But He only said, "Go!"

Three times I confirmed God's call. After this I asked my father, and he said, "Go, and don't come home again. I won't accept you here anymore."

On that day I made my choice. I started walking. For four months I walked, often sleeping outside in the cold. I didn't know where to go, or why, but I kept going in obedience to God. Often I had no food.

Then one day, I entered a particular region, and God spoke to me: "Wherever you set your foot in this region, you will win souls."

That was the direction I needed! Shortly after I began ministry in this area, a leper came forward for prayer. He was cured and then wanted to be baptized. He took on a new name, *Naaman*, and many more villagers were eager to accept Jesus after they saw this.

The church began growing. Next there was an 80-year-old woman with bone cancer. We fasted and prayed for her, and she was renewed and healed. Others started praying and seeing healings as well. God was working among us! One woman died during a colon surgery, and our church went to pray for her. She had small children, and we decided to give our time to praying for her and for them. After one hour, she sat up and was restored to life and health! These miracles led many people to come to our church.

In 1997 India Gospel League helped us construct a Life Center. We had many crowds and had to expand our meeting space. With IGL help, we started conducting eye camps to assist those who need glasses or have vision problems. Thus far we have hosted 115 of these events! Many political leaders come and participate in such things, and we are able to give them Bibles.

Today we have sixteen branch churches, and we have outreaches in prison and the hospital, to fishermen and lepers, and we also share Christian books. There are sixty women's groups meeting now for Bible study and practical life training. We hope to expand all of these things.

Pastor Kumar went on to share his vision with me, which included more skills training centers, a children's home, a pharmacy for the poor, a home for the aged, a widows' home, and of course, more churches. Despite the prosperity of Pastor Kumar's ministry, he maintains the humble life that reflects the way his village lives. "I have no house for sleeping. We sleep in the children's church area. Many people have no houses in our region. They have huts. I want to have the same life as they do so I can have a testimony to them."

OUR WITNESS

What does Pastor Kumar recommend for those of us seeking to serve God?

"If we speak with prayer, if we talk and move in prayer, God will work. This has been my experience. Then, throw your net, they'll come in, then catch them. If you can't catch the fish, you have to go deeper—by kneeling. When I started, I had no single dollar. Many, many days I had no food. Many days I would eat leaves or drink farm water. Many days God fed me miraculously. But I am not in poverty. Now I get to feed many. I do not ask for money. My God is a rich God. With Him I am richer than . . . Bill Gates!"

He was laughing, though tears were in his eyes. "Nothing is too hard for the Lord. What is impossible with man is possible with God."

Pastor Kumar asked if I would pass this message to believers in the U.S.A.: *"If the Christian people work hard, very soon God will turn the U.S.A. upside down. America will bring billions into the kingdom of God."*

———————————

DISCUSS IT

These stories seem to reflect directly what is in the four Gospels and in the book of Acts. Why do you think God is doing miracles today in the young churches of India?

What lessons can you draw from these stories regarding your own life or your own church?

Referring to Pastor Kumar's last statement about the U.S., what do you think it would look like if our churches decided to work hard? How might it play out in your personal life?

ACT ON IT

Write down your testimony of how God has worked in your life thus far. Have a friend help you edit it so it sounds good to you for sharing with others. Then pray over your story. Ask God what He would like to add to it in the future.

SHARE IT

Before God changed my life, I was . . .

Barefoot pastors of central India, having walked to a small leadership meeting from nearby mountainside villages.

A woman in Tamil Nadu offers the traditional Indian greeting as we enter her village.

A young woman leads children in a Bible study, a part of IGL's Children's Gospel Club program.

CHAPTER 7

TESTIMONIES

W hat is daily life like for a Christian in rural India, and what does that have to do with *how* the Great Commission is being carried on there right now? The best descriptor I can think of is to imagine camping at a state park on a holiday weekend, multiplied by a few million people.

This comparison came to my mind at 4:30 a.m. one day when a loudspeaker (emphasis on *loud*) kicked on at a local temple and started blaring Indian love songs. There was a festival that day, and the townspeople were eager to get things going. Celebration was in the air, right along with the cool morning dew. If you like crowds, festivals, animals, and spices, you'll love India.

Later that day, as I rode in a van to a regional pastors' conference, I thought of the thousands of people we passed by, kilometer by kilometer, and tried to pray for those I saw. Every man and woman I saw has dreams, hopes, families, failures, and struggles. Every one of them needs the love, forgiveness, and joy of a relationship with God. Seeing these vast numbers of people milling about in marketplaces gave me a different vision of John 3:16.

"For God so loved the world, that he gave his only Son, that whoever believes in him should not perish but have eternal life." The world is a bigger place than I had realized, and, by extension, the love of God must be bigger as well. In India today, there are 1.3 billion reasons Jesus stayed on the cross when He could have come down and ended His suffering. And each face I saw along the street was one of them.

But how will they know? Who will tell them about the love and grace of Jesus? Allow me to share a few more testimonies, just a sample from among the thousands of stories we can hear more fully in heaven someday.

PASTOR ANIL—EVIL SPIRITS AND LEPERS

Pastor Anil preaches in villages that have been held captive by fear to evil spirits for generations: "A god who demands your blood, what can we call him? A demon? But Jesus never asked for your blood. He gave His own for you. Other gods have killed people, but Jesus came to save sinners."

Every Friday Anil's congregation meets for fasting and prayer. During these meetings many come for healing, and many put their faith in Jesus. Since 1998, they have celebrated 950 baptisms.

His ministry began after Bible training with IGL. He went to a remote area, going house to house, serving lepers, preaching the gospel. Today, his first work has spawned more than thirty-five new places of direct ministry. He has trained seven "junior pastors" and, through Vision 2000, is launching various women's and children's ministry works as well.

PASTOR AMOLIK—BEATEN BUT NOT BROKEN

When Pastor Amolik encouraged me in a conversation with him to "be holy" and to "be faithful to the end," his words carried with them the weight of experience. He said:

> Even though my parents were very strong idol worshippers, I still saw a lot of sickness around me. I saw a Christian prayer meeting one day, and I saw people getting healed. I went, and the pastor was giving a Bible series from Genesis through Revelation. He explained the plan of God, how humans can be saved from destruction. At that point I decided to give my life to Christ.
>
> Since 1997, I have seen God do many things. Evil spirits have been cast out. More than 750 have become Christians. I have been able to train 28 new pastors to go out and start churches. Through IGL's Children's Gospel Club program, I've been able to help introduce many children to Jesus Christ as well.
>
> Some Muslim families have come to the Lord in recent times, although in our church, 75 percent of the people are converts from Hinduism. In 2004 I faced some opposition from people who were very unhappy about our work. Five men caught me and beat me because I was converting Hindus to Christ. I spent four days in the hospital recovering. My friends warned that these people would come back and kill me. But I have prayed and continued on.

PASTOR MARKAS—FROM BUSINESS TO MINISTRY

From birth I was a nominal Christian, and I only went to church on special holidays. I was a business owner. In the year 2000, I had a number of problems in my life and business. Pastor Anil was conducting a prayer meeting nearby, and I wasn't interested. But because no one else would help me, I went and asked for prayer. Slowly, I started going to church, but I was shy and would sit in the back of the room. Soon I was attracted to the ministry and started trying to emulate Pastor Anil's life.

After this I went for Bible training. For six years now I have been ministering, and people are joining my church from all kinds of backgrounds, mostly Hindus who are now trusting in Christ. We now have sixty-five members! In my former business I could make a lot of money, but now I can serve the Lord. Anyone new that I meet I try to pray for that person and bring him to Jesus. Every week, my wife and I conduct fasting and prayer on Friday, Saturday, and Sunday for our church. Recently our people were able to collect enough money for us to start building a church to meet in.

Many people (even pastors) run after money. My challenge is for people go to places where no one has ever shared the gospel, where people need the light. When we do this, the Lord will bless us.

PASTOR BRAKASH—GO WHERE NO ONE WILL

I became a Christian as a boy, and I started doing ministry work when I was nineteen. I was doing medical and social work in villages, but I saw some disturbing things that my fellow ministry workers were doing, and I knew they weren't right. I was frustrated by this hypocrisy, and I left the ministry.

Instead, I got a job at factory. One day when I went to work, I thought a particular machine had been turned off, and I touched a component that was still on. Thousands of volts of electricity shot through my body, and my clothes started burning immediately. I only had time for one thought, "Lord, have mercy on me, I give my life to You!"

I fell down, my whole body burned, and those who saw me thought I was dead.

Yet somehow, the Lord rescued me, and I knew what I had to do. I ended up in a Christian meeting led by Sam Stephens, and he gave a message about God's call. It was for me.

I left my factory job and came back again to ministry; now I do it full time. I started going to remote villages where no one else wanted to go. Since then, two hundred people have been baptized, and my son has just completed his training to be a pastor as well. Together we have work going in seven places. I challenge people all the time to go where no one else will go, to the unwanted and the poor.

PASTOR RAJA—SAYING YES

Pastor Raja, one pastor in India with whom I have a special bond (I'll share the story in chapter 11), is a servant of Christ in a farming region of southern India. When he was in twelfth grade, a Christian lady came to his village and prayed for him. As she prayed, Raja saw a strange vision—that of himself standing up and speaking before a crowd about Jesus! Here is his testimony:

> At that time, I had a job in a factory, and I really didn't understand how this vision would happen. Soon I understood that I was supposed to be a pastor, but I resisted. I even said, "God, let me keep making money, and after I have enough, I will serve You."
>
> But He called me, and I obeyed. I quit my job and started with nothing but the clothes on my back. I didn't want to tell my family about this decision, so I kept it from them for a while. My ministry was difficult. No one liked me at the beginning. When my parents learned what I was doing, they were very angry. They shouted, "Raja if you are in ministry, who will take care of us when we are old?"
>
> My wife spent much time in prayer, "lifting her hands to the Lord" just like Moses had to keep his hands up. Then, God opened doors in our village. God did miracles. And in the meantime, all our needs were being met. In fact, I am even able to care for my parents! Our church is growing, and we are glad to serve God where we are. Today our church

is a part of India Gospel League's Adopt-a-Village program, which is bringing a lot of development and help to our people.

When faced with challenges, a lot of people only see the problems. But we need the faith to see not just the situation, but *God's ability to change the situation.*

LIFESTYLE EVANGELISM

Pastor Anil works with lepers and those who are captive to evil spirits. Pastor Amolik works with Muslims as well as Hindus, and he has withstood being beaten severely for his boldness. Pastor Markas was a business owner. Pastor Brakash was a factory worker who nearly lost his life, and now he challenges people with his story to "go where no one else will go, to the unwanted and the poor." Pastor Raja has the gift of faith, to "see not just the situation, but *God's ability to change the situation.*"

What about you—your gifts and talents? How can your unique testimony open doors for you to be a Great Commission worker?

God has called each of us to live our lives for His purpose and no other. The story He is telling though your life is *His* story. And like our brothers and sisters in India, you were designed to bring glory to God every day, through the choices you make and the places you go.

———————

DISCUSS IT

Have you ever faced a threat for preaching the gospel? If you did, how would that change your faith and your witness?

How can believers discern if God wants them to remain in their occupation or to leave it to do full-time ministry?

In your personal ministry, what would it mean for you to "go where no one else will go"?

ACT ON IT

In your local community, where is the place that no one else will go? A place of deep need? A place where crime runs rampant? A place that is uncomfortable? A place where there is no earthly hope? Begin praying for and learning about ministries in that place. Ask God if and how you can serve.

SHARE IT

One person who really inspires me to live the #gospel is . . .

From businessman to church planter, Pastor Markas struck me as quiet, serious, and committed to Christ.

The natural beauty of India is stunning, from classic jungle to more arid regions, as this picture from near Nasik illustrates.

Sara works with IGL's Adopt-a-Village program, assisting, training, and encouraging women leaders in many villages throughout the southern tip of India.

CHAPTER 8

REACHING PARADISE

W ouldn't it be nice if God called you to be a Great Commission worker in some warm, tropical, exotic place? I'll be perfectly honest: If someone told me I'd have to spend the rest of my life on *Sri Lanka*, I'd be *thrilled*. It is as beautiful an island as any I've seen. Sweeping views of palm fields, surrounded by stunning mountains and pristine lakes, a growing economy, and warm sea breezes—it's basically the definition of tropical paradise.

The island has two people groups, the Singhalese and the Tamils. (The latter share a cultural heritage with the Tamils of southern India.) Both people groups are numerous on the island, though the Tamils are the minority class and are prohibited from positions of influence or ownership. This disparity is the cause of a twenty-five-year civil war that began in 1983, and though it is officially over, there is still suspicion and danger. Many believers on the island have stories that intersect with this dark period of violence. But in deep darkness, light shines brighter.

All of these challenges are compounded by the fact that the population is divided between Buddhism and Hinduism—

both very different philosophies of life, purpose, and spirituality. So who is qualified to carry the message of Jesus into this diverse cultural context? After a short plane flight over the Gulf of Mannar and a six-hour van ride through interior Sri Lanka, I was about to find out.

DIFFERENCES AS STRENGTHS

Pastor Ranjith had a disarming smile and a gentle demeanor, and his wife, Sarojah, was beaming as they told me about their ministry, past and present. He was Singhalese, she was Tamil. So we had no shortage of comedy trying to communicate, since my translator was Tamil. Ranjith would relate a sentence in Singhalese, Sarojah would translate it to Tamil, and then my Tamil translator would share it in English. We enjoyed a lot of laughs and "clarifications."

When Ranjith was about twenty years old, he was a broken man, addicted to alcohol and disappointed with this life. The expectations he did have about his adult life had been crushed by circumstances, so he was lonely and frustrated, and his heart was filled with hatred.

In his mind, the only answer was suicide. So he went to a railway line to wait for the 9 p.m. train, intending to lie down on the tracks and end his life. In his final moments, he started to think, "If there is any true, loving God out there who can reveal Himself to me, then I will not do this. Otherwise, since there is no one to love me, I will die."

Just then a stranger on a bicycle road across the track, looked back at Ranjith, and smiled. Out of courtesy Ranjith smiled back, which caused the man on the bike to stop. The stranger said, "Sir, I know why you are standing here. I know that you are going to kill yourself at the 9 o'clock train. But I want you to know there is a loving God named Jesus, and I'd like to tell you about Him!"

This prophetic stranger then shared Matthew 11:28, "Come to me, all you who labor and are heavy laden, and I will give you rest." Ranjith's mind was racing! He kept hearing that verse again and again. "Someone is going to give me *rest*?" So he followed the man to a nearby gospel meeting, heard the message, and accepted Jesus as His Lord that very day.

For three months he hid his decision from his devoutly Buddhist family. When they learned of his conversion, they forced him to choose between Christianity and remaining in their home. If he would not return to Buddhism, he would have to leave. He chose Christ, of course, and ended up in the home of a nearby pastor.

Soon Ranjith was on his own road to the pastorate, and during his training he met his wife, Sarojah. From here, they would begin a life of ministry together. God provided richly during the early days. They both were attending Sri Lanka Bible College, but they ran out of funds. Miraculously, just before leaving, they were notified that someone had paid their whole two-year tuition cost!

The college gave its graduating students of that year a choice of twenty-five unreached villages to which they could go and plant a new ministry. After three days of fasting and prayer, God told Ranjith which village he must go to—a place he had never been and knew nothing about.

His Singhalese training pastor tried to change his mind. Finally the pastor said, "If you come and work with me in our area, I'll give you monthly support. But if you go to this new place, you'll be on your own."

So Ranjith went on his own with no support, and spent his first night in the bus station. There had been unrest in the area, some killings and riots, so when he approached a home asking for water, he didn't realize there was a rebel group inside. They immediately believed him to be a spy and pulled a gun on him, to which he said, "No, no, I'm just looking for water, and I'm doing ministry here!"

Then God gave Ranjith the ability to do for these rioters what that stranger had done for him on the railroad tracks. Ranjith started to talk to them about *their* lives. As a result, they invited him to stay for three days. He was able to share with them that what they were doing was wrong—that killing was a sin, and that the gospel offers a different way of life. They listened, and he said, "With God's help, you can escape from this party, this rioting." They all prayed and trusted in Christ!

One of these twenty-four men said, "Pastor, you are welcome to stay at my home whenever you wish." So for the first year of Ranjith's ministry in this new village, he would stay in the home of this believer each weekend. Then, Ranjith and his wife were allowed to stay in that house as their own, rent-free, for two years! They didn't have any money or support, but all of their needs were met except for food.

As wonderful as this provision was, the lack of food started to weigh on Sarojah. She said, "I cannot continue like this, so I will go back to my parents' house for some time and come back." But that very night there was a knock on the door, and a lady brought food for them! It was their first good meal in more than a month.

These provisions continued, and the ministry grew as well. Before long, ten children were living with this couple, and fifty believers were gathering in their home for worship. They received help from India Gospel League to begin constructing a small church building.

The work of Ranjith and Sarojah soon caught the attention of the Buddhists in the area. "You cannot build a church here. You are converting people!" One night, an angry group destroyed the frame of the in-construction building and set fire to Ranjith's kitchen.

The couple was not dissuaded from their calling. They found a place on the outskirts of town where they could build a new church. Someone they had never met (from the country of Lebanon) heard of their plight and bought the land on their behalf. In 1998, they were invited to join the Vision 2000 movement, and through this network the funding for their church building was provided.

"Since the Vision 2000 movement encouraged us to plant one new church every year, we have done that," Ranjith reported.

"We have planted eight branch congregations around our church. We have trained up about twenty new pastors to send to Bible school. Some of these lead their own churches now. We have more than 500 people worshipping Christ in the area God led us to years ago!"

Ranjith and Sarojah had one child and adopted four more in the course of time. All of these have pastoral ministries of their own. Their daughter has a significant women's ministry in the region to train and encourage ladies. Today, Ranjith and Sarojah look at each other affectionately as they discuss the next step of their dream together, to help churches grow. They've started travelling to new congregations in the region, spending two days with them at a time, teaching, sharing ideas, and serving as IGL regional coordinators for Sri Lanka.

Every question I asked this couple seemed to uncover more stories of God's power and the growth of their ministry over the years. They summarized in this way:

> What we have achieved is not with our own strength, but by His power. We are nothing. He is everything. Please pray for us as we train more disciples and send them to plant more churches. And pray as we go to encourage at least one other church per month.
>
> We started with nothing. No friends, no money. Only God was our help. We believe with God everything is possible. With God we started, and with God we continue. We go with God, and God can meet our needs. We want to encourage you to

follow and have faith in God, and He will take care of you. We never asked anything from others, but God helps us through others. We have a theme for our churches: "With God all things are possible."

MISSION BASES

Pastor John, another of IGL's regional Sri Lankan leaders, hosted me in his home for a delicious, home-cooked meal. If you've never sampled cuisine from South Asia, I must say, you're missing out. The home was open-air, with nothing more than orange curtains in the doorways. The whole experience reminded me of the reasons I have grown to love this part of the world, but more, the people of God, no matter what nation they are in. What an amazing feeling to share fellowship with John's family—to look past our cultural and language barriers and see a common commitment to Jesus Christ. (I don't think non-Christians realize what they are missing, nor do many Christians, who are too busy with lesser things to forge friendships among God's family worldwide.)

Today Pastor John leads a mission base in Sri Lanka. The base includes a pastor training center, homes for forty-eight orphaned boys, and more. But his story begins in 1986, when he was arrested by the Sri Lankan army on suspicion of terrorism. After John had spent two years in prison, a pastor was arrested—Pastor Ambrose—and put in the same prison. At the time, John was only 17 years old, and he heard the gospel from the pastor, recognized his sin, and prayed for God's transforming power in his life. Here is how he recounts what happened during his and Pastor Ambrose's imprisonment:

Twenty-five other inmates trusted Jesus as well. The prison guards were impressed by our change of heart and decided to buy us all Bibles. Pastor Ambrose taught us and even made us take turns preaching to one another!

At that time I wanted to be a preacher of the gospel, and I prayed. The Holy Spirit told me, "I am going to give you the gift of preaching!" Soon, there was a political agreement for our release, and when I walked out of that prison, I made a decision: "I will do God's work!"

God has grown Pastor John into one of the foremost servant leaders of the Sri Lankan church. When I asked about his vision, he said, "We are hoping to train and send forth fifty new pastors each year. We are looking to build more mission bases, skill centers, and church buildings throughout Sri Lanka."

REFUGEE CAMP MINISTRY

Whenever and wherever people are displaced, there is great opportunity for ministry. Refugee camps where people find temporary asylum from war and natural disasters are "open doors" for the gospel and humanitarian assistance.

In 1994, crippled Pastor Morgan was in a refugee camp in India, having fled with his family from the Sri Lankan civil war. He found Christ in the camp and began his discipleship training. Soon the government took him to another refugee camp in India, where a thousand families lived. Here's his story:

There was no minister there, so I began sharing the gospel! I was praying over people and preaching the gospel one day when I realized something strange was happening—God was healing me! My crippled leg was restored to full health, and I started walking and jumping and running! "God has healed me!" I yelled.

I kept feeling my leg to verify that this was all real. The people in the camp saw this miracle, and it became my testimony to them of the power of God. Soon the Vision 2000 movement provided us with a prayer shed, a small building where the growing congregation could meet. I remember one day in particular when thirty-nine people were baptized!

We quickly outgrew our shed and applied with the government to build a church. They denied our request. So, since we could not grow bigger in the camp, we started to train our men to head into the jungle to start new ministries in nearby villages.

In 2003 God told me to go back to Sri Lanka. At this time I had four children, who were all in school. We had a good congregation, and all our needs were met. But I had a very vivid dream. Our whole family was flying to Sri Lanka, coming back to my own place. When I woke up, I prayed, "Lord, is this real? If You confirm this, I will tell my church." I went to back to sleep, and I saw this whole dream again!

I got advice from other pastors, and all of them confirmed this action. I told my church. I started trying
to go back to Sri Lanka, but I fell and was not able
to walk. So I told my congregation, "When I came to
India, I was handicapped. Maybe I am supposed to
return to Sri Lanka that way!"

DISASTER RELIEF MINISTRY

Have you ever felt God's Spirit tug at your heart to go to a
place that has been devastated by a natural disaster such as
a hurricane, tornado, or flood? Pastor Morgan's continuing story shows us how God calls and uses His workers in
times of disaster.

When he heard God speak to him, Morgan left everything in
India, believing that God would provide for his needs in Sri
Lanka. He told the people when he arrived in his village that
he would not ask for anything, that God would give all that
was needed. He prayed, "Lord, wherever You lead me, I will
go. Show me the place." He recounts what happened next:

I had another dream. The Lord showed me a very
specific piece of land in the foothills, and later I
found out that this place actually existed and that
it was available! We had no money, but my wife and
I prayed together. We went and walked around on
the land, praying. Shortly thereafter, a large sum
of money was given to our family. We immediately
bought the land and started our new ministry.

Only one person came to church on our opening day. But soon, four or five families joined us in worship. By 2004, we were ready to do an ocean baptism with seven new believers.

On the morning we'd scheduled the baptism, we had planned to go to the ocean first and then come back for services, but at the last minute we felt like we should rearrange our schedule. We stayed in the church instead of heading to the beach. Shortly thereafter, we saw people running and yelling. A massive tsunami had hit our island!

Our church immediately started to serve and help anyone we could. Even though we didn't have anything, we went and talked and prayed with those who were suffering near the coast. In one village, ninety people were killed.

We immediately began making longer-term plans to assist people in rebuilding, replanting, and resettling. What we planned opened the hearts of our community to us, and, amazingly, the government actually gave us a church building to use.

Today more than two hundred people worship in our church, and we've trained five leaders to do ministry in surrounding areas. This year we have set a goal to touch a hundred families with God's love. We divided our church into three groups to work on this vision. Our hope is to plant more churches.

God gave me one more unexpected blessing. One day
my children were gathered around me praying, and,
praise God, my crippled leg was healed a second time!
Today I walk normally!

EVEN IN THE MIDST OF WAR

Sometimes we have no idea how God will use us, particularly
when the darkness around us seems overwhelming. Yet, for
the next pastor I interviewed, God had used him in some of
the worst situations imaginable.

When I was small boy, Jesus used me in a mighty
way, but because of disobeying Him, I lost my way.
I did many sinful things. But my life was changed
when a snake bit me and the doctors told me that
I would die. And they were right. For nearly fifteen
hours, there was no life in my body. I was dead.

During this experience, Pastor K.S. explained, he saw his life,
his direction, and most of all, Jesus. He repented and gave his
life back to God. Upon regaining his health, K.S. immediately
enrolled in Bible school and started looking for opportunities
to minister. (This was during the civil war.) He did ministry
in places where the war was raging. Here is his testimony in
his own words:

At one point, officials came and took our church
youths to force them into military service. As our
children turned seventeen, we were forced to hand
them over, even our daughters.

In the course of being moved around and forcibly relocated, I ended up with a thousand believers around me, looking to me for leadership. I remember one Sunday we were together praying, and the Spirit told me to get out of that building immediately and move. I obeyed, and moments later, the entire area where we had been meeting was bombed.

We went to another place, and there, while I was preaching, I heard a voice saying, "Take your people and leave quickly!" So we all had to leave again, and within ten minutes, that place was also destroyed.

Another time, we were surrounded by "Tigers" (the rebel forces) so, I knelt to pray. They came to kill me. I had to run and hide. Later that night, I took my group, which had now grown to 1,500, and tried to escape into a government army area. The Tigers found us and were trying to persuade us to join them, when government troops appeared and opened fire! Twenty-four of our people died, and fifty-five were wounded.

Four of my own family died in that place during that battle. I had been standing with a Sri Lankan flag to identify with the government troops, yet my wife and children ended up standing closer to the enemy flag holder. We could not get to one another across the field of live battle. A government soldier told me, "If you go over there, we will shoot you." But I had to go.

A sniper saw me moving toward my children and began firing. I prayed, "God, save me! Guard me!" He did. I wasn't hurt. I made it to my family, and shortly thereafter, the battle was over.

After a year, the government took us back to our land. Everything had been lost. Everything had been broken and destroyed. But again, we began ministry. Today, our ministry has about five hundred new believers. We have set a church goal to share the gospel with a hundred thousand people, five hundred of whom we pray will join our church community in the near future.

I asked Pastor K.S. if he had any words of encouragement for believers elsewhere in the world. His message was concise: "I believe this is the end of days. Every believer, *go to Jesus*. Do something for God's kingdom." Amen.

PERSECUTION BY FIRE

The Bible speaks of persecution as an expected part of sharing the gospel. Jegan's story offers us hope when our witness is rejected or when we encounter major obstacles.

Jegan was a terrible drunkard and smoker; in his words, a "problem-creator, a fighter." His mother and father hated him, so he left home and lived with friends and, sometimes, on the street. He awoke one day to realize a painful reality: *Everyone* hated him. He had no future. On a regular basis, he thought of ways to end his life.

A friend of mine who knew about my life finally asked, "Jegan, what are you doing? Would you like to change?" He told me that someone called Jesus could help.

"There is no way," I answered. "I cannot stop drinking."

My friend assured me, "You don't stop; you give your life to God, and He will help you stop."

He convinced me to attend church with him, and the pastor spoke about these exact things. I was angry at my friend, thinking he had told the pastor my personal story. He hadn't; but my friend said, "God knows your heart. God is the one who created you. That's why God brought you here today, and that's why He is speaking directly to you. Even if no one else loves you, God loves you."

Well, to follow Christ, I had to leave my old friends and allow my new Christian friend to disciple me. God gave me the grace to stop all of my addictions and bad behavior.

One day in my house, I lay down and prayed to God, and while I was praying, I heard God speak. "You live this way because one man came to you and told you about Me. That's why you are living this way today. Look around you. There are many youths who have lost their lives. *Go tell them about Me.*"

At that moment, I told God, "I am willing; I will do it." I gave my life to God's service.

There have been many persecutions. In 2001 I started a ministry in a village, only to have it ruined by Buddhist youths who came and drove our people away. In 2004, twelve of them broke into our house with weapons and ordered me to leave, threatening to kill me and my family. Then they broke everything in our home and burned our things.

After this I never left this area, because God told me, "This is the land I called you to. I am with you." In 2009, again, they burned my church building and home. We didn't even have clothing to wear; we had nothing. But God said, "Don't worry, My son, I will provide."

In spite of these persecutions, today a church congregation of 150 gathers in this area. Pastor Jegan explains, "One thing I know—we are not given an easy job. But if we commit ourselves totally to God's work, He will do what He wants to do. That's the lesson I have learned. In our flesh we can't do anything. If we deny ourselves, then God can use us. We are vessels for Him."

LOVE THE ENEMY

What kinds of resistance have you encountered in your efforts to share the gospel with others? To what extent have you encountered enemies to the gospel and their wrath?

One church planter in Sri Lanka named Sam (not Sam Stephens) came from a Roman Catholic background. He gave his life to Christ as he learned about what a personal relationship with God means. At one point on his journey, he felt called by God to attend Bible school and become a church planter. Here is his testimony:

> I have faced many persecutions. Twice, my church building has been destroyed and rebuilt. At one point I handed my ministry to an assistant and went to another unreached area. The Tigers' power was high there, but I too was a Tamil, so the locals didn't do anything to me. I built a church there, and we saw twenty-four people baptized. Then I started a ministry to surrounding villages.

> The war was raging nearby, and soon widows and injured people started coming to me. I thought to myself, "How can I preach to these people? How can I pastor them?" Then I knew I couldn't leave this place, even with the bombs and bullets flying. I had to stay and share all I could. In that place I had to bury nearly three hundred dead children with my own hands, but God showed me that I would live and continue to do His work after the war.

> Once I shared my vision of peace with the believers—that the war would end. At that time, outside of my house, there were forty bodies yet to be buried. People thought I was crazy for believing that these enemies would ever come to terms. Finally, the

peace came, but not before I had seen so many of my own Tamil people slaughtered. With my own eyes I saw these things.

As we resettled into our own village again, a number of Singhalese people moved nearby. I could never love them, I thought. But one day, when holding an open-air gospel meeting, a number of Singhalese came, and fifteen families were converted! They came to me after the service and asked, "Pastor, can you guide us?"

Now, I could not speak their language, and they only spoke a little Tamil. But even worse, I thought I could never love them after everything I had seen their people do to mine. "You had better go find a Singhalese pastor," I replied.

But there were none in the area. These families appealed to me five times. And five times I rejected them. Then God gave me a dream about the good Samaritan.

At first I thought God had given this vision to the wrong man! But then I realized, *this is about me and Singhalese people.* So I got them together in one place, and we prayed. And in that moment, the thing I never thought I could do, I did. God did. I handed all of my Tamil ministry work to my assistant and resolved to take on the task of pastoring these Singhalese. Now I spend more time with them than I do with Tamils!

Story after story from Sri Lanka confirms something I'd suspected all along—that the ministry vision and Great Commission strategies of India Gospel League could readily be applied in other contexts, other nations, and other cultures. But then again, it's not so much about the "model" of ministry work or the specifics of how it is done, it is really about the power of the Holy Spirit. He alone can transform hearts, bring miracles to pass, and even turn hateful bitterness into pastoral love. That's the kind of power the Spirit makes available to us, wherever we are, from whatever dark place we began, for whatever challenges lie ahead.

_____

DISCUSS IT

What do you think of the husband/wife team of Ranjith and Sarojah? What must it take to maintain such a strong, affectionate marriage in the midst of so many challenges?

If, like Pastor Jegan or Pastor Sam, your church building was destroyed by angry radicals, what do you think your congregation would do? How would you respond?

Share how you have you ministered to someone who was formerly your enemy or who had hurt you somehow.

ACT ON IT

Based on Romans 12:21 and the premise that believers should overcome evil with good, ask God today what person has intended evil for you, or against whom you have held bitterness. Through Christ's love, share a blessing with that person—a gift, a word of encouragement, a gesture of friendship and reconciliation, or an unexpected note of thanks. Then, begin praying for that person's relationship with God.

SHARE IT

One thing I am learning from the book #Commissioned is . . .

Sri Lankan hospitality, extended to us by our hosts at one of IGL's mission bases near the east coast. Yes, I had seconds.

IGL provides Sri Lankan pastors with magazines, teaching aids, and children's curriculum to assist in spreading the gospel.

Pastor John and his wife provide leadership and encouragement to many church leaders; they also manage a mission base that provides a home for 48 boys in need.

CHAPTER 9

TRAINING YOUNG LEADERS

W ho are today's leaders? Who will carry the message of the cross to upcoming generations? What do these leaders need from us to fulfill their calling?

To Daniel Stephens, son of Sam Stephens and director of India Gospel League's youth training division, today's leaders are the 18–25-year-olds. "Tomorrow's leaders," he adds, "are children under the age of 16."

Danny himself is evidence of this, who from an early age would travel with his father doing village-to-village ministry, and who, after graduating from Bible college, has rejoined the ministry. Today, Pastor Danny's role includes, among other things, the task of mobilizing and training 50,000 of *today's* leaders to lead IGL's annual children's outreaches to more than 600,000 of *tomorrow's* leaders. *Yes, that math is correct.* Fifty thousand young people trained to be part of an annual outreach to 600,000 village children. (One thing I've learned in India is to add a few zeros to the end of any vision. Remember the multiplication of the churches described in chapter 2?)

Children's Gospel Clubs (CGCs) are akin to Vacation Bible School meetings, only they stretch forward for a year of weekly discipleship groups. Through this outreach, hundreds of thousands of village children receive not only the gospel but also a year-long journey through the Bible's core teachings. Many of the Vision 2000 church plants are host locations for this massive effort.

The work of Danny, Benny, Sam Stephens, and others of the IGL leadership team reminds me of the famous statement by Henrietta Mears, founder of Gospel Light Publishing: "There is *no magic in small plans.* When I consider my ministry, I think of the world. Anything less than that would not be worthy of Christ, nor of His will for my life."

The scale of India Gospel League's vision for reaching the next generation would be unbelievable to me, had I not seen it personally. These dedicated workers set goals that really are worthy of Christ—they rely on the provision of God and plan to make tangible advances toward the completion of the Great Commission.

LEADERSHIP TRAINING PRINCIPLES

Behind all these big numbers and bold visionary statements are some simple leadership training principles that are passed along to every person who joins in the ministry of IGL. I had a brief opportunity to watch Sam lead a training session with about thirty young pastors on how to train others. It was intensely practical, and about midway through, I started to wonder why the U.S. seminary I'd attended hadn't spent more time teaching me to think in these terms. Sam had identified eight elements for the growth of the church:

authentic spirituality, outreach, worship, Christian education, preaching, leadership development, missions, and administration.

He asked each person to write these elements down and determine what specific steps they would take to grow in each one during the next twelve months. Then, how would these ideas be implemented and measured?

On the first element, authentic spirituality, he spent some time discussing personal disciplines. Then he suggested each person set some specific, church-wide goals. For example: Identify twenty-four Bible characters, and have the congregation study one character per month for two years. Another example: Identify twelve spiritual disciplines, and make each one a monthly discussion for one year. He explained, "This is measurable. This is realistic. And after three months, you could ask your church, 'How is this helping you? Is this working? Are lives changing?'"

Then Sam discussed the second element, evangelism, and asked the trainees to say how they might approach it. He gave them this *specific, measurable* example: "I will select six believers to train with six lessons on evangelism; then I will take each of them out to a village and show them how to do it."

After discussion, Sam continued with the third element, worship. He said, "Worship is more than what happens in the first few minutes of our Sunday service. We must not think that if we clap our hands, sing songs, or get emotional for about ten minutes, we have finished our worship. The Bible teaches, and we know, that worship is much, much more than that. So how do we develop worship in our congregations?" He challenged those being trained to write down ideas they had and to pray about them after they returned home.

Sam continued his teaching, focusing on the fourth element: "The next element of church growth is Christian education. It is very important for believers to grow on the foundation of strong doctrine. But that cannot happen only through preaching. We need to teach them through Bible studies and small groups. And, since it is not possible for you to teach every single person, we need to develop people who can teach others. We see that in 2 Timothy 2:2."

This goal is easier said than done in India's rural villages, where the literacy rate is extremely low. Sam admitted as much to the group. "For nearly two-thirds of our believers, reading the Bible is difficult. It is very important that they *hear* these teachings. So what can we do?"

One eager trainee spoke up with an idea: "We could teach one person in each family to lead their own family in prayer and Bible study!"

Sam replied, "I like that. Great idea. Very good. But even with this, let me encourage you to be more specific in terms of a goal. Would you do this once every month? How many people will you train each month, and how will you accomplish that?"

The next element he discussed was preaching. Sam's words still ring in my ears:

We as pastors need to be able to stand in front of our congregations and confidently say, "This is a message from the Lord for you." To do so means you need to schedule hearing God as a high-priority item in your life. For example, "Every week I will spend six hours preparing and praying for my message."

Sometimes we tend to preach on just one topic all the time. Our preaching gets lopsided as far as doctrines are concerned. So read and prepare balanced messages throughout the year that you can preach. Find different helps and aids to do that. Sometimes through Vision 2000 we can give you a series of message ideas for the Christmas season—outlines you are free to use. You could sit down and pray and ask God to help you plan ahead for an entire year—twelve months of what you intend to preach.

Next up? Leadership development.

What can we do to develop leaders in our congregations? One goal we are setting in front of all our Vision 2000 churches is to train two Women with a Mission leaders, two youth leaders, and two male leaders. What are some specific goals and priorities you can set? For example, if you don't have a leader for your youth, you can't have a youth program. So that should become a priority. Good leadership is the mark of a healthy church.

When Sam got to missions, I wondered how far he would take it. After all, among his audience were seasoned village church planters to the unreached of India. In my mind, they were already living out the mission more than any other group of people I could name. Here is what he told them:

> Every believer must be committed to the fulfillment of the Great Commission. It is not just for a few people; it is for you and for me, and for everyone God raises up under us. You are not only to teach and train, but you are also to create opportunities so all people can be involved.

> We in Vision 2000 have started a program called MAP—Missionary Adoption Program. This means you will get the information about one missionary who is in a difficult area, and your village congregation can pray for that person and give something to their support. Your adopted missionary can come and visit your church, and you can also go and visit your missionary.

> Apart from being involved in local evangelism, your church also needs to look at missions across the world. Remember Acts 1:8? We must go to our Jerusalem, Judea, Samaria, and to the ends of the earth. So how do you create that kind of awareness in your congregation? What can you set as a specific goal?

Sam paused and looked intensely at the faces of his students. "How many of you have been to Jharkhand? How many of you know where it is?" (Only a few in the room responded.) Sam continued.

It is important for you to know where the unreached areas in our county are. You are *leaders*. Your vision must go beyond just where you are. You must know the needs in other places so that God can burden you to meet them. This is very important!

So the first thing you can do is go get a map for yourself. Hang a map of India where you can see it every day, and pray for India. Encourage your believers to pray for the nation.

We have to look beyond our state, our own country. You should even begin praying for other countries.

Do you know that a few years ago, hundreds of our Christian brothers and sisters were killed in the state of Orissa? Shouldn't we have a burden for the believers there? Aren't they part of our family? So what should we do? We are always looking after our own needs and problems, but there are brothers and sisters in deeper need and in deeper poverty than we are. *God wants us to have concern for everyone.*

There are other countries in the world that also do not have the freedom to worship that we have. You think we are going through persecutions and problems, but there are countries in the world where you can get killed if someone finds out you are a Christian. Shouldn't we pray for those countries?

Finally, Sam concluded the eight-part discussion on church growth by considering ways to better administrate the village churches, and the goals that might be set to develop healthy church structures. Then he said, "The next time we come together, we will be looking through these elements again to discuss what you've decided and how you are doing it. That meeting won't be next year. *It will be next month!*"

When the meeting adjourned, I sat there silently for a few minutes. *There it was,* the reason churches are growing, pastors are accountable, and the strategy is working. Into a place where the Holy Spirit is opening doors and doing miracles, into regions where Jesus has never been named, God's leaders in India are *training* their young leaders for *action.*

I left ready to take action myself.

————————————————

DISCUSS IT

Danny's profile of today's leaders is a bit younger than what we may be accustomed to thinking. Why is this? Could the youth in your church be mobilized and trained toward kingdom leadership?

What role do IGL's monthly regional follow-up meetings have on momentum and the continuation of the work? What accountability for progress like this do you have in your church and personal life?

Which of the eight elements Sam discussed in his training needs the most development in your own life? How about in your church family?

ACT ON IT

To be a faithful gospel witness, it is important that we train, prepare, and plan accordingly. Find out what gospel training opportunities exist in your church, and commit to memorize some key verses that will allow you to start speaking up for Christ. *Recommendations from the book of Romans: 3:23; 5:8; 6:23; 10:9-10; 12:1-2.*

SHARE IT

One goal I have for my life this year is to serve God by . . .

The focus on training up young people to serve Christ is central to IGL's ministry philosophy.

A well-worn Bible belonging to a village pastor says more than I ever could about his resolve, vision, and commitment.

Most IGL church planters will begin multiple infant congregations in the first few years of their ministry.

Young village ladies studying the Bible in their own language.

CHAPTER 10

DANGERS TO THE WORK

Not everything is easy about a Great Commission lifestyle. In fact, very little of it is "easy." Rather, it is dangerous, challenging, and demanding! At every turn, there are risks. And in every place, there are spiritual battles beyond our comprehension.

Sam Stephens and the IGL leaders are well aware of the dangers faced by their rapidly expanding network. The stories of persecution, poverty, deception, and struggle in India and Sri Lanka remind me of what Paul wrote to the Corinthians.

> . . . on frequent journeys, in danger from rivers, danger from robbers, danger from my own people, danger from Gentiles, danger in the city, danger in the wilderness, danger at sea, danger from false brothers; in toil and hardship, through many a sleepless night, in hunger and thirst, often without food, in cold and exposure. And, apart from other things, there is the daily pressure on me of my anxiety for all the churches (2 Cor. 11:26-28).

Aside from opposition from radical religious groups and unfriendly local governments, some of the greatest threats to God's kingdom being established in India are surprisingly similar to the threats Western churches face.

CONTROL VS. PARTNERSHIP

One thing Sam is very adamant about is that IGL and Vision 2000 will not become a denomination. The league offers a *voluntary association,* with resources, training, prayer, and encouragement; but it does not *control* the churches or the pastors. The reasons are both biblical and historical, and they offer lessons for us as well.

Historically, India was ruled by Western empires for many generations, which left a deep-seated resentment among the population for outside controllers. (Actually, all of humanity shares this same resentment.) At one point in India's history, all foreign missionaries were ordered to leave the country.

Most denominations present in India in the major cities today are associated with or headquartered in the West, and most of those are a result of long-standing past relationships before the ban of foreign missionaries. Their presence, and new presences from the West being created, means that the wonderful *local* work of God could at some point be in danger of becoming tied to "foreign" groups, just like in colonial days. Such alliances, Sam believes, compromise the witness of the indigenous pastors, and complicate their relationships with the people they are attempting to reach.

To avoid this issue, IGL strictly adheres to an *indigenous* philosophy of ministry, which means *everything* is run by people local to the area, not by Americans or Europeans, and when possible, not even by Indians from other states in India. Indigenous Christian leaders need outside *partnership*, not outside *leadership*. For this reason only, India Gospel League is happy to arrange peer-to-peer partnerships between churches in India and those in North America, Australia, Europe, and elsewhere.

This commitment to indigenous leadership extends directly into the organizational structure of IGL as well. Even though a North American board of directors coordinates partnerships and helps with fund raising and ministry promotion, this group only exists to serve the Indian organization, not the other way around (as is more commonly the case in missionary organizations today).

Sam explains it this way: "With recent geopolitical changes, most of Asia is not where it was. It is less receptive to things that are foreign or imported from the West. These factors need to be identified and adapted to as we talk about missions. Sometimes we are tempted to just use the same old colonial model, but it could have very negative consequences today."

In other words, little could slow the growth of the South Asia church faster than some well-meaning outsiders getting too hands-on. *It is important for us to submit to the leadership God has raised up* for this season in South Asia rather than try to impose our own controls, ideas, or methodology.

DENOMINATIONAL THINKING

Some denominational churches really believe their way is *the* way. And if they come with money in hand, they can wield undue influence on pastors in need of resources. It would be a tragedy if India and Sri Lanka's faithful church planters adapted their methods to fit "outside" expectations in order to receive resources or approval. It could quickly stifle their ministry multiplication. That's why it is so critical to ask how we can best *serve* the Indian church, for example, rather than offer "our plans."

While driving through the middle of Sri Lanka, I had time to ask Sam a few questions about this issue and how to strike the right balance. He put this way.

> One thing I fear for the church here on Sri Lanka, and also in India, is that it would become too Western and not really fit into its cultural context. Right now the leadership of IGL-connected churches is all indigenous. We're working with independent church planters. I fear they could be tempted to mimic what they see in the West or be pulled in by some well-intentioned denominational group.

> The influence of the media makes holding the line on this principle difficult, since the media makes the West's ways look tempting. There are people in the West from a variety of denominations that support IGL, and some even send their pastors over to help with training, but they aren't exercising any authority or control here. This is good. We need partners, not directors.

Personally, even though I come from a non-denominational church, I know there are a lot of good people who contribute to denominational mission groups. So I asked Sam, "In light of what you are saying, what would you recommend that denominational missionaries do? What about the churches that have already been planted in cities here based on the Western way of doing church?"

"Three things," Sam said, glancing out the window at the passing jungle.

First, it is important for them to see what God is doing, the *new move* that is happening here. It is different from years past. So it's a matter of changing your framework for thinking, your idea of what mission work looks like.

Second, we need to be looking carefully at what is developing in the church culture locally. It is so easy to import ideas, methods, and success stories from other places. But God is doing things *here*, and those things should be evaluated and encouraged.

Third, we need to start looking for ways to make the churches here sustainable for the future. Some denominationally attached churches are completely dependent on outside support for their money, leadership, strategy, and resources.

The way the indigenous church is growing now is unprecedented. We may have models from the past, the way missions used to work a generation or two ago, but what is happening *right now* is that churches are being planted, watered, and grown without any outside influence. I think it is important to encourage this.

His words made sense to me, except for one thing. *What was I doing there?* "Couldn't the presence of American guest speakers at training conferences cause problems? People like me really want to help, and we love to give to meet some of the resource needs the church planters have. How can we serve and partner without 'importing' Americanized Christianity with us?" I asked.

Sam shook his head with a smile. "The context is different, Dan. The locals are inviting you, and the team is coming just to encourage, not to administrate. The strategy, the planning, the leadership—all of that is owned locally by the church leaders here. You're not coming to them and saying, 'Here is my model, and I'll give you resources if you adopt it.' You're coming to support their model and encourage them in it."

PROSPERITY GOSPEL

In the West, a host of evangelists and television preachers promise great material blessing from God in exchange for simple acts of faith, prayer, or even contributions to specific ministries. The underlying philosophy is that "God wants you to be happy," and even sometimes, "God's children should always be rich, healthy, and prosperous."

Such thinking is greatly at odds with the teachings of Christ, and it leaves little room for persecution, suffering, or sacrifice. Such "feel good" Christianity is alluring, and was held forth by those Jesus mentioned in Matthew 7, "who come to you in sheep's clothing but inwardly are ravenous wolves" (Matthew 7:15-23).

Imagine importing a so-called prosperity "health and wealth" gospel to a poverty-stricken coastal village in India or Sri Lanka. Not only would it feel initially attractive, but also in the long run, it would prove devastatingly disappointing. Sam identified this "false gospel" as the number one doctrinal threat to the churches. So many village pastors have not been to seminary or training conferences, so they are susceptible to these mistaken ideas. Satellite television is now starting to make inroads even into the rural regions of India, and with it comes the full lineup of both good and bad religious teachers broadcasting from the West.

UNSUSTAINABILITY

I asked one of IGL's staff in Tamil Nadu about the self-sustaining nature of the ministry work. "I know there are a lot of believers around the world who donate to IGL," I said. "What would happen to the work if suddenly all of that were to disappear?"

The answer was encouraging: *The work would continue.* New development would slow down, and many opportunities to minister to children or the poor would be reevaluated. But the core mission of planting churches would continue, because the planted churches are self-sustaining.

This statement gets to one of the most distinctive features of IGL's strategy for completing the Great Commission. Their objective is not to accumulate some vast number of workers that are "supported." Rather, it is precisely the opposite. Support for church planters is only offered for up to two years, and that only to those who truly need it. Many Vision 2000 pastors are not supported by outside funds *at all*.

That's how IGL has been involved in the planting of more than 70,000 churches with only a few hundred full-time workers employed by the organization at any given time. Church planters and their churches aren't receiving a monthly check. They are supporting themselves and multiplying themselves. Some village churches even choose to give a portion of their tithes each month to IGL to serve other Indian congregations.

The rural development work of IGL is likewise built to be self-sustaining. Foreign churches may partner with a very poor village through the Adopt-a-Village program, but the funding part of the relationship only lasts for five years.

Often when outsiders offer to build a church building (Life Center) for an Indian congregation, the field leaders require that church first to give "to the best of their ability" toward the project before outside funds are applied. The same principle holds true even down to acquiring curriculum workbooks and Bibles.

Sam Stephens explained it to me this way:

> If we provided, for example, free Sunday school curriculum to all our churches, which we probably could

do using money from U.S. partners, what would happen to the Sunday school program if we had to stop the support? The church wouldn't continue it. They wouldn't feel responsible for their own Christian education. But because they have to contribute, even if it is a small amount, they are invested in the work. They still know there are partners elsewhere who are helping them, but the relationship is different. They aren't getting a handout. It is *their* Sunday school program.

OUR DANGERS TOO

For those of us who live in the West, the dangers are nuanced differently, but at their core, they are very much the same. Could we be tempted to let others do important work for us? Could we be tempted to buy into a gospel message that is more about our own comfort than it is about God's glory and vision for this world? Could we have leaders who try to build their own kingdoms rather than God's kingdom? Could you and I fall prey to unhealthy denominationalism, and could that slow down the Great Commission work in our culture?

DISCUSS IT

The traditional model of missions involves sending Western believers to foreign cultures to establish new churches. Once these churches are established, it is important for missionaries to yield to the new indigenous leadership. What difficulties would you expect during these transitions?

If you were in Sam Stephens' position, how would you go about protecting infant congregations from the dangers identified in this chapter?

What danger does your church, in your nation, face? What are the top spiritual dangers in your own life?

ACT ON IT

Ephesians 6:10-18 outlines the armor of God that can help you prepare for whatever dangers you face. Look up this text and pray through each item of armor, and ask for God's wisdom going forward.

SHARE IT

The #Bible talks about spiritual battles. That's why I'm praying for . . .

A village congregation fellowships outside its newly constructed Life Center building, following a time of worship and teaching.

Becky Stanley, daughter of Sam Stephens and a leader of IGL's children's ministry outreaches, hands out Tamil Scriptures to villagers, following a baptism service.

Two men share greetings, a pastor and his former persecutor, now at the same pastors' conference.

Pastors Manova and Benny, both involved in
training church planters and teaching theology.

CHAPTER 11

NEW FRIENDS

With tears in his eyes, an intense Sri Lankan man looked at me, clasping my hand as we parted. *"I feel like you are my good friend!"* We had spent a few afternoons together; he had served as my translator as I collected stories of God at work from pastors in the region. I felt the same surge of emotion he did; the likelihood of us ever seeing each other again (until heaven) is admittedly slim. But in those few days, we had formed a bond of friendship. Even more, I think, across our cultures we had really seen what it is to bond together for the cause of Christ.

Pastor Prag's journey of faith began in 1989, when he received a horoscope that said his baby daughter would die quickly. The prediction continued that if she did live, she wouldn't walk or talk. At the time, Prag was a Hindu priest, a holy man working in a temple, worshipping idols.

On October 21, 1989, I went on a small journey, and two men saw me. They stopped and told me about Jesus Christ. I asked them, "Do you have anything further I could read about this Lord?" They gave me a New Testament, which I started reading as soon as I got on the bus. That is when God spoke to me: "I have chosen you!"

Over the next seven days, I read the entire New Testament three times. I shut all the doors in my house and just kept reading, and then I heard someone calling my name. But no one was there. After this, I got this unknown fear, and anytime I closed my eyes, I felt some darkness surrounding me like a snake or a shadow. I could only get relief by praying and holding my Bible close to me. I didn't know how to pray to Jesus, so I just started saying His name. "Jesus, Jesus!"

My wife saw me like this and told our neighbors, "My husband has gone crazy. He is always taking this book and calling out, 'Jesus, Jesus.' He is not doing the normal worship of our gods, but he is going to rooms and closing the door, and I don't know what he is doing!"

Finally, a man named Pastor Moses came to our area and really explained the Bible to me. Both my wife and I became Christians, and both of us were baptized. My daughter was fine. In fact, we've had other children since then.

Well, immediately my conversion created problems in our village. After all, I was their priest! The people told me, "Since you are not working in the temple, we will stop giving you money." But I held on to

Jesus Christ. I started frequently going to church. And God provided for us. On August 18, 1999, Pastor Moses completed his training with me, and my church anointed me as a pastor.

Since then I have seen many people healed from diseases and demonic forces in the name of Jesus. God gave miracles to my ministry. In August 2012, I prayed for one girl I knew could not speak or hear for eleven years. She immediately began to talk and hear! Nearly thirty-eight demon-possessed people have been set free. Today I am the pastor of six churches, and in just the last month, forty-seven more believers have been baptized. One hundred nineteen children attend our Sunday school.

Today Prag is writing a thesis as part of his schooling on Christianity in Sri Lanka. He and the team he has built have reached forty-two different areas with the gospel.

I asked Prag to share a little about his vision for the future. He didn't even blink before answering: "That each and every place here on the island would have a church planted." He explained his plans to help street beggars, to share with them, and to give them a simple message: "The Lord Jesus loves you." This simple statement comes in striking, shining contrast to the fear-based, ritualistic faith most people observe. And to the outcasts? "You are loved— loved with an everlasting and gracious love, the personal love of Jesus." And Pastor Prag is sharing this good news with as many as will listen!

"How can I best pray for you?" I asked, "apart from some specific ministry requests regarding the new church work, outreaches to children, and so on?" Prag grew intense in his plea when he explained, "We don't have a fight with human beings, but with demonic forces. We have to teach people to go out with the gospel. We must stand firm—faithfully, truly, holy, with all that we are—to do this work. It is a great privilege to serve God. He is doing marvelous things in the world."

He offered me this encouragement, from the book of Jude: "But you, beloved, building yourselves up in your most holy faith and praying in the Holy Spirit, keep yourselves in the love of God, waiting for the mercy of our Lord Jesus Christ that leads to eternal life."

Then Prag looked straight at me with eyes full of tears. "The Lord God is choosing us from the dust for *His* work, not our work. With our last breath, we are to run to Him. That is my vision; that is my hope."

That moment is one of many times in meeting God's faithful servants in that faraway land that causes me to choke back tears. I can't shake the power of Prag's vision. Would I too one day run to Christ with my last breath? As if I had served and shared and preached and lived the gospel right up until my last ounce of human energy was spent and then turned to the Savior's welcoming arms, drawing a final gasp, fleeing toward Him as I escape this ruined world?

Prag is just one among thousands of pastors God is raising up across India and Sri Lanka under similar circumstances. It is an honor that I can call him my good friend.

ONE UNFORGETTABLE INDIAN

From Prag's region, a six-hour car ride, a one-hour plane flight, and another six-hour car ride brought me to a small village in southern India. It was a village I had seen once before, a village being transformed by the gospel one life at a time.

Through India Gospel League's Adopt-a-Village program, my wife and I and other families from our church have partnered with Pastor Raja to assist in bringing the gospel and a host of humanitarian helps to this particular area. Since our first encounter in 2009, a sewing skills center has been established to train women with job skills; children's educational programs and family hygiene initiatives have been launched; a few village women have gone to college (an unheard of development for lower caste villagers); and many people have been reached through community Bible studies. All of this, and most importantly, the growth of Pastor Raja's church congregation.

I think about this small village on a near-daily basis, and when I do, my prayers and thoughts revolve around Pastor Raja, his beautiful family, the many smiles of villagers whose lives have been changed forever by the work of the gospel, and the sight of scores of eager children receiving education and a real chance at forging a better future, *beyond caste, beyond expectations.*

Pastor Raja has also seen God's power at work. Once, when the village well had run dry, the believers gathered to pray and saw the water rise back to a normal level.

But more than the healings and miracles that might be noted here are the testimonies of changed lives stamped in my memory from my visit that day. Like the deaf girl who never thought she could do anything productive, who wondered as she grew up what would become of her. (There aren't many good options for handicapped citizens in Indian villages.) Today she is a joyful follower of Jesus and a graduate of the sewing center. She wrote a letter to be read aloud for us that underscored her gratefulness.

Another woman shared with me her story of hopelessness turned to peace through Jesus. "I never thought this kind of life would be possible for me," she said, as tears streamed down her face. Children shared their stories as parents cried in delight. Three of the young women from the village were heading to nursing school. Life and joy had been introduced into the lives of people who, just a few years ago, had felt little more than pointless despair and personal depression.

Of course, I was hearing all these things through a translator, but the tears, the smiles, and the emotions of that day were hard to misinterpret. God had done great things among them. The blessings of the gospel were richer than any in the village had expected. And despite the hardship suffered by those who walked away from their traditional Hindu roots in order to embrace Jesus, His grace has made the journey worthwhile. He is, after all, *the way, the truth, and the life.*

What a joy it is to know that one more of India's 600,000 rural village communities is being reached through the hard work of Pastor Raja, supported by the many servants who comprise India Gospel League.

The visit was made complete by an unexpected surprise. A few of the women in the village had delayed their baptism so that they could share this special moment with me and those traveling with me. It was a day of celebration and testimony of all that God had done over the past few years.

There was no formal baptistry or backyard swimming pool. Instead, the church gathered at the bank of a large river, just downstream from a Hindu temple, to witness these three young women make a public profession of their lifelong commitment to Jesus. And public it was! Along the shore people gathered (most of whom were not Christians) to see this curious Christian "ritual." In fact, a group of men walked up to one of the believers and started to ask questions about the Christian faith. Maybe this was the original intention of *public* baptism.

When the crowd dispersed, one man stayed behind. He had studied Hinduism and Islam, and he had heard of Christianity but didn't know anything about it. He asked the believers for help, and they happened to have an extra Bible in the man's native language, right there in hand! He went home with a broad smile and instructions to read the Gospel of John and then to call Pastor Raja if he wished to discuss the faith further.

Such is the hunger in a land unreached with the gospel. Such is the bold witness of the Christians there, in villages, in cities, in marketplaces, and in baptisms along the riverbanks!

By then it was sunset, and time for us to leave the river and once again disappear down the road, away from the village, away from these dear believers, away from those who in the past few years had grown to mean so much to us. Although we live as far apart as possible in this world, we share the same vision and the same Savior. Just as I have pictures I treasure of Raja's family and church, so too a picture of us hangs on the wall of a small rented meeting space in his village. They pray for us regularly, as we do for them.

In a final parting gesture, Pastor Raja grasped my hand in friendship, and with tears rolling down his cheeks, wouldn't let go. He kept repeating, "Thank you. Thank you. Thank you."

No, don't thank me! Thank Christ for joining us together in His Great Commission. Thank Jesus for His power, working through each of our lives, as we follow Him.

———————————

DISCUSS IT

If you could offer an encouragement to church planters like Pastor Prag or Pastor Raja, what would you say?

When and where have you experienced friendship "in the gospel" as is illustrated by these stories? Where else would you like to form friendships with believers from other cultures?

India Gospel League calls its overall work "holistic" because it leads out with the gospel but then assists wherever possible with the practical needs of the villagers, as illustrated by the Adopt-a-Village program. Why do you think this holistic approach is important?

ACT ON IT

In your circle of friends, who could partner with you in the gospel work? With whom could you imagine working and praying, side by side, to advance God's kingdom?

Today, contact those individuals and ask about meeting with them to discuss opportunities you could take on together for the Great Commission. Next, look past your own culture. Pray about forming a global partnership such as was illustrated in this chapter.

SHARE IT

Jesus' last earthly words were the #GreatCommission. He calls us to . . .

The believers at our adopted village, dedicating a new facility that helps poor women receive training to manufacture clothing and start their own businesses.

Pastor Raja encourages young believers in preparation for their riverside baptism.

Back at the village, children assemble ahead of a testimony service to share all that God has been doing among them in the past few years.

CHAPTER 12

EXPECT GREAT THINGS

William Carey was a great missionary hero of Christian history. He was a pioneer—a missionary before it was popular to be a missionary. In fact, after pleading with a ministers' gathering in England to take personally the Great Commission, William was famously interrupted by an older (and obviously cranky) pastor: "Young man, sit down! When God chooses to convert the heathen, He will do so without your help or mine!"

Carey, a shoemaker, hung a world map in his shop and prayed for the gospel's advance in faraway lands. He felt God's call to take the message personally to India. In the economy of his day (late 1700s), this meant leaving the comforts of home, enduring a long sea voyage, putting to shore in an area unfriendly to the gospel, and having no insurance and very little assurance that things would work out or that he would ever see his home again.

To add to the difficulty, Carey's family and friends thought he was insane and tried to talk him out of going. His wife initially refused, but Carey plodded on. She grudgingly agreed to join him, but later in his ministry she literally went mad and tried to kill him after one of their sons was taken with a tropical fever. He faced tremendous financial setbacks, resistance from governments, sicknesses, and dangers. Like the apostle Paul, Carey was "afflicted in every way, but not crushed" (2 Corinthians 4:8).

Time would tell, however, that Carey's ministry was one of the most influential in history, inspiring generations of missionaries in the West and jump-starting a vibrant church presence in India. Carey translated the entire Bible into Bengali, Sanskrit, Hindi, and other tongues; and he translated portions of Scripture into more than thirty dialects. Some of his translations are still in popular use today. At the same time, he also labored to create dictionaries for these languages, translating classical Indian works into modern dialects. He rejoiced to see Indian believers holding freshly translated Scriptures in their hands for the first time, the name of Jesus penetrating the unreached subcontinent.

Carey also founded a college (in his free time, no doubt), helped secure social reforms in India (such as banning *sati*—the burning of widows on their husbands' graves— and outlawing child sacrifice in sacred rivers), and started a newspaper entitled *Friend of India*. His mission station in Serampore became a model for missionaries the world over, earning him the title "the Father of Modern Missions."

While Carey himself never saw the full fruit of his labor, it can be said today that millions have been led to Christ from the seeds he planted in the late 1700s and early 1800s. His tireless devotion to Christ and to the people of India changed that nation and, because of the extended influence of his missionary challenge, changed the world.

Carey's motto was as well known to his associates as it is today in missionary circles: *"Attempt great things for God; expect great things from God."* He could have prayed over his world map in England and stopped there, continuing to make shoes and hoping God would somehow do the work. But Carey did both—he prayed, then attempted something that seemed impossible.

A WORKABLE STRATEGY

Things are obviously different now. We live in a different time. India has different needs. Because of the seed-planting work of previous generations, the premium isn't so much on getting more "William Careys" to set sail for India. Today the need is to *partner* with the Christian leaders already there, already serving, already sharing.

Even though the church has been established, and even as we report the amazing growth experienced by IGL and other similar groups, we have to set all of it in perspective. *Most Indians still are unreached with the gospel.* Only a miniscule percentage of India's nearly 1.3 billion people even claim to be Christian.

The most cost-effective, sustainable, and proven way to reach these lost millions in our lifetime is to stand alongside Sam Stephens, and other leaders like him, and offer the best of our financial and prayer support. The front-line workers in India and Sri Lanka already speak the language, they already know the customs, they already live a village lifestyle, and they've already been called by God to serve. All they need is training, prayer, and resources to move forward, farther and faster than they could on their own.

With or without us, they'll labor hard for the gospel. But we have before us an eternal opportunity that I wouldn't want to miss. God is working in South Asia, and whatever we can do to support the vast harvest there, I'm ready.

There are other areas of the world that still need traditional missionaries, gifted and called specifically for a certain time and a certain place. And sometimes, most times in fact, God calls us to do things that don't make sense on paper. But as far as it depends on us, we should approach the missionary task strategically in our time, just as William Carey did in his. *That means we need to recognize what God is doing and join Him in that work!*

A COMMISSION COVENANT

In 1805, William Carey wrote a covenant for his missionary team that still rings true for any of us who are seeking to complete the Great Commission, in India or elsewhere. It shed light on the kind of commitment, heart, and sacrifice required to lay the groundwork for kingdom advancement. He and his team agreed to:

1. Set an infinite value on people's souls.

2. Acquaint ourselves with the snares which hold the minds of the people.

3. Abstain from whatever deepens India's prejudice against the gospel.

4. Watch for every chance of doing the people good.

5. Preach "Christ crucified" as the grand means of conversions.

6. Esteem and treat Indians always as our equals.

7. Guard and build up "the hosts that may be gathered."

8. Cultivate their spiritual gifts, ever pressing upon them their missionary obligation, since Indians only can win India for Christ.

9. Labor unceasingly in biblical translation.

10. Be instant in the nurture of personal religion.

11. Give ourselves without reserve to the Cause, "not counting even the clothes we wear our own."

This is an abridged version of Carey's covenant, the full text of which is available in the 1884 edition of *A Short History of Christian Missions*, by George Smith. I know it is easy to skim over lists like this without really digesting what they contain. But look back at Carey's words. Are we willing to be as strategic and thoughtful as he was, when it comes to our mission from God? Are we giving ourselves without reserve to the Cause, seeking God's kingdom above all else?

WHAT'S WRONG?

On my return trips from India, I've wondered why it seems like "God is on the move" in one place but not so much in another. Why are there miracles in India? Why is the church growing at such a fantastic rate? Why are hundreds of thousands of people seeing the light of the gospel? If there is a Great Awakening on one side of the planet, why not on my side, in North America?

Certainly the problem isn't with God. He's the same, on one side of the planet or the other. In fact, the more I search the Scriptures, the more I see compelling evidence that God wants to do His great work in every nation, among every people, and with every generation. Consider His Word:

> [God our Savior] desires all people to be saved and come to a knowledge of the truth (1 Timothy 2:4).

> He commands all people everywhere to repent, because he has fixed a day on which he will judge the world in righteousness (Acts 17:30-31).

> Jesus Christ the righteous . . . is the propitiation for our sins, and not for ours only but also for the sins of the whole world (1 John 2:1-2).

There is no distinction between Jew and Greek; for
the same Lord is Lord of all, bestowing his riches on
all who call on him. For "everyone who calls on the
name of the Lord will be saved" (Romans 10:12-13).

All the ends of the earth shall remember and turn
to the Lord, and all the families of the nations shall
worship before you. For kingship belongs to the Lord,
and he rules over the nations (Psalm 22:27-28).

Now to him who is able to strengthen you according to my gospel and the preaching of Jesus Christ,
according to the revelation of the mystery that was
kept secret for long ages but has now been made
known to all nations, according to the command
of the eternal God, to bring about the obedience of
faith . . . (Romans 16:25-26).

The Lord is . . . patient toward you, not wishing that
any should perish, but that all should reach repen-
tance (2 Peter 3:9).

That's all the evidence I need! God's promise—the power of
the gospel—is just as available to me in my context as it is to a
village pastor half a world away. God's intentions for transformation are global!

All of this has led me to recommit myself to His purposes:
"Yes, God, I will honor You with all I have and with all that I do.
I don't fully understand Your ways, but I do desire to obey You
fully. Wherever You lead, whatever I must give up, wherever
You send me, I'll go. I'll believe. For eternity, I'm Yours."

Jesus is on the move, redeeming and rescuing sinners everywhere. The same God who can restore sight to the blind is the one who can restore vision to your Christian life. The same God who did impossible miracles in Bible times is ready to do impossible miracles through all who have faith in Him. He's working in India today in ways I scarcely have words to describe. I yearn for the day when this can be said of my country and my culture as well.

A CHALLENGE TO WORK HARD

I do have a theory. While interviewing so many Indian and Sri Lankan leaders for this book, I noticed two recurring themes: These servants of Christ *really* pray, and they *really* work hard. I don't want to reduce all of the complexities and mysteries of how I saw God moving in India to such a simple paradigm, but I do wonder about it. What if we all laid down our excuses and started praying faithfully and doing exactly what Jesus said to do? Would His presence and power be felt among us as well?

Every story of spiritual power, every healing, every village-wide conversion, every miraculous provision—these are happening to people who are out on the front lines making sacrifices every day. The Spirit is most at work among those who are working hard for the gospel.

I shared this challenge with a friend in the U.S., who was a bit taken aback by my terminology. "I don't usually hear about *working hard* for the gospel." I wonder why not? The apostles certainly worked hard for the gospel, until their last breath (literally). Paul wrote about his "toil" and "struggling" in sharing the message (Colossians 1:27-29), and he asked the Ephesians to pray that he would remain a bold proclaimer (Ephesians 6:19). There was even a woman Paul commended in Rome "who has worked hard for the Lord" (Romans 16:12).

We're told to work hard at school. Work hard at our jobs. Work hard at investing for retirement. Work hard to gain a good reputation. Work hard at raising our children. Perhaps even work hard at Bible study. But what about working hard toward the completion of the Great Commission? What about working hard to let the whole world know about the life-changing power of Jesus? What about working hard as a laborer in the harvest field, the way William Carey did? What work, I wonder, is more important than this?

Yes, this could mean rearranging our priorities. It could mean challenging our churches to look up and see the vast harvest God is bringing in. It could mean going out to reach people that no one else wants to reach, serving the poor and the needy, caring for the orphaned or the sick. It could mean partnering with groups such as India Gospel League and giving all we can to make a difference. It could mean allocating significant time in our schedules to prayer. It could mean starting outreach teams and taking evangelism classes. It could mean sharing the gospel with the people God has already put into our lives. Much of this will be hard work, accomplished by God's grace and with the power He provides.

If we will work hard for the gospel, we *can* expect great things. If we start with the humility and love of Christ in our heart, if we take every step forward with prayer, if we yield to the Spirit's leadership of our lives, we can expect God to move. We can join God in His great work of transforming the world, one life at a time, until Jesus comes again.

So let's do it, my friends. Let's be the witnesses the Spirit has empowered us to be. Let's make disciples of all nations.

You and I have been, in a word, *commissioned*.

———————————

DISCUSS IT

Which of Carey's eleven covenant points surprise you? Which would you have the hardest time maintaining if you were serving on his team?

What are your thoughts about the Great Commission being completed in your lifetime? What will this vision require of you?

What great things has God been prompting you to attempt for Him?

ACT ON IT

Like William Carey, find a world map or globe you can use as a reminder for prayer about the global work of the Great Commission. You might even ask something bold like this: "Lord, You've planted me in my city, in my home, for a reason. How can I best use every skill or gift I have to share Your gospel? And how would You have me reach across the world, to those who have never heard?"

SHARE IT

Because I read #Commissioned, I'm planning to . . .

A field laborer, tending to his duties.

One of more than 70,000 congregations planted by IGL. Jesus is indeed building His church!

The future of the Christian movement, on the floor of a tiny church; learning to pray, learning God's Word.

A PERSONAL NOTE

In chapter 1, I suggested that this book is an *invitation*. Not just to *know about* something great God is doing, but an invitation to be a part of it.

I took Sam Stephens at his word when he said, "Come and see!" and it changed my life. You can do so as well. A few months from now, you could be meeting the church-planting pastors of South Asia, just as I did. You could be an eyewitness to one of the greatest spiritual movements in history.

I'm now committed to share every resource I can with my friends in India and Sri Lanka. Sponsoring pastors and children and villages and even regions through IGL has become a passion of mine. Would you be willing to join me in that? There is so much work left to be done. There are millions of families that need to be reached. Your partnership could lead literally thousands more to encounter Christ's love. The resource pages to follow offer all the specifics you'll need to begin.

I'd love to hear your story of how God has used this book to engage you in Great Commission living. To find me, contact

IGL's North American office at *www.IGLworld.org or email info@iglworld.org.* They can forward your message to me, and I'll do my best to respond personally and answer any questions you may have. And I will certainly pray for you, as a fellow worker in the gospel, wherever you are in the world, sharing Jesus boldly.

Attempting and expecting great things from God,

Dan Jarvis

APPENDICES

APPENDIX A

FIRST STEPS OF INVOLVEMENT

Would you like to partner with India Gospel League and the efforts of Vision 2000? Christians from all across the world give time, energy, and financial resources to support the work of Christ in India and Sri Lanka. Here's how you can jump in:

1. BEGIN PRAYING FOR SOUTH ASIA. You might consider printing a map of India and becoming familiar with its states, people groups, and geography. Articles on specific needs, cultural challenges, and news updates are posted at www.IGLWorld.org. If you'd like to pray for people around the world, consider the book *Operation World* by Patrick Johnstone. A wealth of information regarding the unreached people groups in India is available at www.JoshuaProject.net.

2. SIGN UP FOR RESOURCES. When you visit the IGL website, be sure to request that your name to be added to the print and email lists. You'll be kept in the loop on new developments from India and exciting ways to get involved personally. Link up with IGL on social media to get up-to-the-minute updates and also to easily share IGL projects with friends.

3. START A SPONSORSHIP. You can fully support a barefoot pastor for $100 monthly, for a two-year commitment (or a one-time $2400 contribution). You'll receive a picture of the pastor and his family along with information about the ministry your sponsorship is making possible. On a quarterly basis, IGL will send you updates on new villages being reached, testimonies from your pastor's ministry, and personal prayer requests. You may also choose to sponsor needy children, adopt whole villages for transformation, and, if you're interested in large-scale projects, adopt an entire unreached region involving hundreds of pastors. *To begin, visit www.IGLWorld.org or call the North American office at 888-352-4451.* (All contributions are tax deductible and are processed via the North American office in Hudson, Ohio.)

4. ORDER EXTRA COPIES OF THIS BOOK. Help spread the challenge by sharing this book with friends and church leaders. Using the discussion questions, you could lead a small group or reading club through this material.

5. GET YOUR KIDS ENGAGED IN MISSIONS. Children's Gospel Clubs reach more than 600,000 Indian children annually. The cost of materials to add one more child to that number is just $1.00. This low amount makes it a great partnership option for kids. It's a great way to give young hearts a global, Great Commission vision!

To give you an even better picture of the scope and depth of the IGL ministry, **videos and audio interviews** are posted on the IGL website so you can get to know the team, see and hear stories of God's power, and grow your vision for what God is doing.

APPENDIX B

COSTS OF MINISTRY (in USD, as of 2014)

India Gospel League has a number of specific projects that donors can contribute toward; or, if you desire, you can always contribute to the general fund, which allows funding to the areas where Sam Stephens and the team need it most on an up-to-date basis. Specific information regarding handling of funds, strict accounting procedures, and accountability structure is available at the IGL website.

The IGL team is excited to present these projects not only because of their effectiveness in sharing the gospel and serving the needy, but also because of their cost effectiveness. For example, supporting an IGL church planting pastor is *more than fifty times less expensive* than sending in a missionary from overseas.

Here is a breakdown of individual project costs:

- Sponsor a church planter (barefoot pastor) for two years
  $2,400 ($100/month)

- Sponsor an orphaned or needy child for one year
  $360 ($30/month)

- Sponsor a Bible school or nursing student
  $50/month

- Build a Life Center (construction materials for a block building) in a village
  $8,000

- Send a village pastor to a training conference
  $55

- Send a "Women with a Mission" worker to a
  training conference
  $55

- Send a child to Children's Gospel Club for one year
  $1

- Build a clean water well
  $1,250

- Adopt-a-Village
  $1,250 per month for 5 years ($75,000 total)

- Adopt-a-Region
  $250,000+ (call for information)

- Meal for a leper colony
  $350

- Chickens (25) and a coop for a poor family to start farming
  $100

IGL has over fifty specific project lines like those represented above, reflecting the four key areas of ministry (evangelism and church planting, children's ministry, medical outreach, and rural development). You can view a whole catalog of opportunities at the website (www.IGLWorld.org).

APPENDIX C

GLOSSARY OF KEY TERMS

Adopt-a-Village – the program facilitated by IGL that helps a rural village experience blessings like medical care, skills training, education, and economic development, all facilitated through the local Christian church recently planted in that village.

Barefoot Pastor – a church planter who works in the rural villages of South Asia, often literally barefoot as he travels village to village sharing the gospel and establishing churches.

Holistic Ministry – ministry to the whole person, not just physical needs but emotional and spiritual needs as well.

India Gospel League (IGL) – an organization based in Tamil Nadu, India, that has been involved in church planting, children's ministry, medical outreach, and rural and economic development.

Indigenous – local, native, also used to describe IGL's structure and leadership.

Gospel – the good news of God's redemptive plan for sinful humanity; what Jesus did by dying on the cross for our sins and rising from the dead on the third day, defeating sin and death and providing new, eternal, abundant life to all who repent and put their faith in Him (see John 3:16; Romans 1:16; Acts 20:21).

Great Commission – the concluding commandment of Jesus' earthly ministry, sending His followers out to make disciples across the world (see Matthew 28:19-20 and Acts 1:8).

Life Center – a village church building, constructed not only for worship services but also community programs, child care, skills training, and more.

Missionary – someone commissioned to share the gospel of Jesus: an ambassador of God's message to the world.

Mission Base – a strategically located property where IGL can train regional leaders, host conferences, care for needy children, and extend compassionate care to nearby communities.

Partnership – a peer-level interaction working together for a common goal. For IGL, partnership involves connecting believers across the world to help complete the Great Commission.

Regional Leader/Coordinator – an individual who serves as an encourager for independent pastors in a region, connecting churches with resources and opportunities afforded by IGL and the Vision 2000 movement.

Sam Stephens – the current president of India Gospel League, serving in that capacity since 1988, when his father passed away.

Sharon Gardens – the first mission base of India Gospel League, located in Tamil Nadu. Sharon Gardens includes children's housing, skills training facilities, a nursing college, a community college, a hospital, an elementary school, a conference center, and guest housing.

Self-sustaining – churches and ministries that do not require foreign donations or leadership to thrive.

South Asia – India and neighboring nations.

Vision 2000 – a network movement of pastors throughout South Asia that have committed to plant churches in unreached villages.

West/Western – a descriptive term pertaining to the North American or European lifestyle; in contrast to the East, which refers to places such India or China.

APPENDIX D

HOW TO LEAD A MISSION-FOCUSED PRAYER MEETING

PRAYER PART I: THE LABORERS NEEDED (Luke 10:1-3)

- for the great harvest in South Asia and the church planters needed

- for IGL and their regional leaders in India that will assist these planters

PRAYER PART II: THE SENDERS OF THOSE WHO WILL PREACH (Romans 10:9-15)

- for many individuals and churches worldwide to join in this strategy

- for adequate resources and training for these pastors to be effective

PRAYER PART III: THE FAITH OF THE CHURCH PLANTERS (Ephesians 6:10-20)

- for boldness in the face of opposition

- for clarity of direction from God and of sharing His Word

- for strength and grace to do their work

PRAYER PART IV: OPEN HEARTS IN INDIA (2 Corinthians 4:3-6; 2 Peter 3:9)

- for the 1.3+ billion Indian people, mostly Hindu and Muslim

- for the many people groups without a Christian witness or Bible translation

- for a continuance of the spiritual revival and church growth now occurring

PRAYER PART V: CELEBRATION OF WHAT GOD WILL DO (Psalm 22:25-31; Revelation 7:9-12)

- the Great Commission must be completed in our generation

- those with the gospel today must finish the task Jesus gave us to do

- God has given us the honor of participating in His plan

CONCLUDING FELLOWSHIP

Idea: If you have more than five participants, you can break into smaller groups of three or four for a few of the above sections to mix things up and give all individuals a chance to pray aloud.

INDIA GOSPEL league

1521 Georgetown Road, Suite 305

Hudson, Ohio 44236

888.352.4451

www.IGLWorld.org

Contact IGL to receive updates, join the prayer team, sponsor a pastor, support a project, or for information about traveling to India.

ABOUT THE AUTHOR

Dan Jarvis is a pastor, author, and conference speaker on a mission to share the life-changing truth of the Bible. After traveling throughout the United States with Life Action Ministries and serving in the pastorate for more than twelve years, Dan now serves in a leadership role at Life Action, casting vision for revival and spiritual awakening; whenever possible, he also assists India Gospel League with advancing Great Commission partnerships throughout North America. He is the managing editor for *Revive* magazine, a publication that helps believers seek God and His kingdom.

Dan is a graduate of Moody Bible Institute and also holds a Master of Divinity in Pastoral Leadership from Liberty University. Most importantly, Dan has been joyfully married to Melissa since 2004, and together they have foster parented more than thirty children. They live in Michigan with their six children and enjoy parks, swimming pools, Mexican food, and traveling through life together for God's glory.

www.danjarvis.us // Twitter @danjarvisus